Raising Resilient Sons: A Comprehensive Parenting Guide For Boys With Dyslexia

Barley Nicola

Published by Barley Nicola, 2024.

RAISING RESILIENT SONS: A COMPREHENSIVE PARENTING GUIDE FOR BOYS WITH DYSLEXIA

First edition. April 2, 2024.

ISBN: 979-8224468867

Written by Barley Nicola.

Table of Contents

Chapter 1: Introduction

- UNDERSTANDING DYSLEXIA in boys

Dyslexia is a common learning disability that affects an individual's ability to read, write, and spell. While dyslexia can affect people of all genders and ages, it is often more prevalent in boys. Understanding dyslexia in boys is important for educators, parents, and caregivers who may work with children who have this learning disability. By recognizing the signs and symptoms of dyslexia in boys, early interventions and supports can be put in place to help them succeed academically and socially.

Boys with dyslexia may exhibit a range of symptoms that can vary in severity. Some common signs of dyslexia in boys include difficulty with phonological processing, which is the ability to hear and manipulate sounds in language. Boys with dyslexia may struggle with rhyming, identifying syllables, and blending sounds to decode words. They may also have trouble with phonemic awareness, which is the ability to recognize individual phonemes, the smallest units of sound in language.

In addition to phonological processing difficulties, boys with dyslexia may struggle with reading fluency and comprehension. They may read slowly and inaccurately, have difficulty remembering and understanding what they read, and struggle with spelling and writing. Boys with dyslexia may also have poor working memory, which can impact their ability to hold onto and manipulate information in their minds. This can make it challenging for them to follow multi-step directions, remember important details, and organize their thoughts.

It is important to note that dyslexia is not a result of lack of intelligence or effort. Boys with dyslexia are just as capable as their peers, but they may need additional support and accommodations to reach their full potential. Dyslexia is a neurobiological condition that affects the way the brain processes language, and it is often genetic in nature. Boys with a family history of dyslexia are more likely to have the condition themselves.

Early intervention is key in supporting boys with dyslexia. The earlier dyslexia is identified and addressed, the greater the chances of success in overcoming the challenges associated with the learning disability. Educators and parents play a crucial role in recognizing the signs of dyslexia in boys and providing appropriate interventions and supports. This may include specialized instruction in reading, writing, and spelling, the use of assistive technology, and accommodations in the classroom.

In addition to academic interventions, boys with dyslexia may benefit from strategies to support their social and emotional needs. Dyslexia can impact a child's self-esteem and confidence, as they may feel frustrated and discouraged by their difficulties with reading and writing. It is important to provide boys with dyslexia with positive reinforcement, encouragement, and praise for their efforts and progress. Building a supportive and nurturing environment at home and at school can help boys with dyslexia thrive and succeed. By recognizing the signs and symptoms of dyslexia, early identification and intervention can be put in place to help boys with dyslexia succeed academically and socially. With the right resources, accommodations, and support, boys with dyslexia can reach their full potential and thrive in school and in life.

- Challenges faced by boys with dyslexia

Dyslexia is a common learning disability that affects the way individuals process and understand language, often making it challenging for them to read, write, and spell accurately. While dyslexia can affect people of all genders, boys are disproportionately affected by this learning disability. Boys with dyslexia often face unique challenges in the classroom and in their everyday lives, which can impact their academic performance, social interactions, and overall well-being.

One of the primary challenges faced by boys with dyslexia is difficulty with reading and writing. Reading requires the ability to quickly and accurately decode words, which can be especially challenging for individuals with dyslexia. Boys with dyslexia may struggle to recognize and understand letters and sounds, leading to a slow and laborious reading process. This can make it difficult for boys with dyslexia to keep up with their peers in the classroom and may result in feelings of frustration and low self-esteem.

In addition to reading difficulties, boys with dyslexia often struggle with spelling and writing. Dyslexia can impact a person's ability to accurately spell words and organize their thoughts on paper. Boys with dyslexia may have trouble with grammar, punctuation, and sentence structure, making it challenging for them to effectively communicate their ideas in writing. This can be particularly frustrating for boys with dyslexia, as writing is a key skill that is often required in school and in many aspects of everyday life.

Another challenge faced by boys with dyslexia is difficulty with memory and processing information. Dyslexia can impact a person's working memory, making it difficult for individuals to retain and recall information. This can affect boys with dyslexia in the classroom, as they may have trouble remembering instructions, retaining new vocabulary, or recalling information for tests and exams. Boys with dyslexia may also struggle with processing speed, which can impact their ability to keep up with the pace of classroom instruction and complete assignments in a timely manner.

Social challenges are also common for boys with dyslexia. Dyslexia can impact a person's self-esteem and confidence, making it hard for boys with dyslexia to feel comfortable and accepted in social situations. Boys with dyslexia may also face stigma and misconceptions about their learning disability, which can lead to feelings of shame and isolation. It is important for teachers, parents, and peers to be aware of the challenges that boys with dyslexia face and to offer support and understanding to help them navigate social interactions and build positive relationships. It is important for educators, parents, and peers to be aware of the challenges that boys with dyslexia face and to provide support and accommodations to help them succeed. By understanding the difficulties that boys with dyslexia face and offering them the necessary resources and assistance, we can help these individuals reach their full potential and thrive in the classroom and beyond.

- **Importance of resilience in overcoming dyslexia**

Dyslexia is a neurodevelopmental disorder that affects an individual's ability to read, write, and spell. It is a common learning disability that can have a significant impact on an individual's academic and professional success. However, it is important to recognize that dyslexia does not have to be a barrier to achieving one's goals. With the right support and strategies, individuals with dyslexia can learn to overcome the challenges they face and thrive in both their personal and professional lives.

One of the key qualities that can help individuals with dyslexia succeed is resilience. Resilience is the ability to bounce back from setbacks, adapt to change, and persevere in the face of challenges. It is the capacity to overcome adversity and achieve personal growth in the process. For individuals with dyslexia, developing resilience can be particularly beneficial in navigating the obstacles they may encounter in school, work, and daily life.

Resilience can help individuals with dyslexia cope with the frustration and self-doubt that often come with struggling to read or write. It can give them the strength and motivation to keep trying, even when faced with difficulties. Resilience can also help individuals with dyslexia develop effective coping strategies, such as seeking support from teachers, parents, or professionals, and advocating for accommodations that can help level the playing field.

Furthermore, resilience can help individuals with dyslexia develop a growth mindset. A growth mindset is the belief that intelligence and abilities can be developed through effort and perseverance. It is the opposite of a fixed mindset, which sees abilities as innate and unchangeable. By cultivating a growth mindset, individuals with dyslexia can approach challenges with a positive attitude, view mistakes as opportunities for learning, and embrace the process of improvement.

Another important aspect of resilience for individuals with dyslexia is building a support network. Having a strong support network can provide encouragement, guidance, and practical assistance in overcoming challenges. This network may include family members, friends, teachers, tutors, therapists, or other professionals who can offer assistance and understanding. By reaching out to others for help and support, individuals with dyslexia can strengthen their resilience and increase their chances of success.

In addition, practicing self-care and mindfulness can help individuals with dyslexia build resilience. Taking care of one's physical, emotional, and mental well-being is essential for managing stress, anxiety, and fatigue that may come with dyslexia. Engaging in activities that promote relaxation, such as exercise, meditation, or hobbies, can help individuals with dyslexia recharge and rejuvenate. Mindfulness practices, such as deep breathing, visualization, or body scans, can also help individuals with dyslexia stay focused, calm, and present in the moment.

Furthermore, setting realistic goals and celebrating achievements, no matter how small, can help individuals with dyslexia build resilience. By breaking down tasks into manageable steps and monitoring progress, individuals with dyslexia can build confidence and motivation. Celebrating accomplishments, whether it's completing a reading assignment, mastering a spelling rule, or achieving a high grade on a test, can boost self-esteem and reinforce a sense of achievement. By developing resilience, individuals with dyslexia can build the strength, confidence, and determination needed to navigate obstacles, advocate for themselves, and achieve their goals. Through cultivating resilience, individuals with dyslexia can turn setbacks into opportunities for growth, setbacks into opportunities for growth, and challenges into triumphs. It is important to recognize that resilience is a skill that can be developed and strengthened over time, through practice, self-awareness, and support from others. By harnessing the power of resilience, individuals with dyslexia can unlock their full potential and lead fulfilling and successful lives.

Chapter 2: Recognizing signs of dyslexia in boys

- COMMON SYMPTOMS OF dyslexia

Dyslexia is a learning disorder characterized by difficulties with reading, writing, and spelling. It is a common condition that affects individuals of all ages, but it is often first noticed in children who are learning to read. While dyslexia can vary in severity, there are several common symptoms that may indicate the presence of the disorder. These symptoms can manifest in a variety of ways and may affect different aspects of a person's life.

One of the most common symptoms of dyslexia is difficulty with reading. Individuals with dyslexia may struggle to accurately decode words, which can lead to slow and labored reading. They may also have trouble recognizing familiar words, which can make reading comprehension a challenge. Additionally, individuals with dyslexia may have difficulty with phonological awareness, which is the ability to recognize and manipulate the sounds of language. This can make it hard for them to sound out words or accurately spell them.

Another common symptom of dyslexia is difficulty with spelling. Individuals with dyslexia may have trouble remembering the correct spelling of words or may mix up the letters in a word when writing. This can make written communication a challenge and may lead to errors in spelling and grammar. Dyslexia can also affect a person's ability to write cohesively and express their thoughts clearly. Individuals with dyslexia may struggle to organize their ideas and may have trouble with sentence structure and grammar.

In addition to difficulties with reading and writing, individuals with dyslexia may also experience challenges with other academic tasks. For example, they may struggle with math concepts that involve sequencing or understanding word problems. Dyslexia can also impact a person's ability to follow multi-step directions or remember information presented orally. These difficulties can affect a person's academic performance and may lead to frustration and a lack of confidence in their abilities.

Beyond academic challenges, dyslexia can also affect other areas of a person's life. For example, individuals with dyslexia may have trouble with organization and time management. They may struggle to keep track of assignments, appointments, and deadlines, which can lead to feelings of overwhelm and stress. Dyslexia can also affect a person's social interactions, as they may have difficulty with verbal communication or understanding social cues. This can lead to feelings of isolation and can impact a person's self-esteem and sense of belonging.

It is important to recognize that dyslexia is a neurodevelopmental disorder that is not related to intelligence or effort. Individuals with dyslexia may be just as intelligent and hard-working as their peers, but they may need additional support and accommodations to succeed academically and in other areas of their lives. Early identification and intervention are key in helping individuals with dyslexia overcome their challenges and reach their full potential. By understanding the common symptoms of dyslexia and providing appropriate support, we can help individuals with dyslexia thrive and succeed in all aspects of their lives.

- Early intervention for better outcomes

Early intervention refers to the timely and proactive measures taken to address and mitigate potential risks or challenges faced by individuals in various aspects of their lives. This concept is often applied in fields such as education, healthcare, and social services to support individuals in reaching their full potential and preventing or minimizing negative outcomes. Research has consistently shown that early intervention can lead to better outcomes for individuals across the lifespan, from childhood to adulthood.

In the field of education, early intervention plays a crucial role in addressing learning difficulties and ensuring that students receive the support they need to succeed academically. This can include interventions such as individualized education plans, tutoring, and specialized instruction aimed at addressing specific learning challenges. By identifying and addressing these issues early on, educators can help students build a strong foundation for future academic success. Research has shown that students who receive early intervention for learning difficulties are more likely to catch up with their peers, perform better in school, and develop positive attitudes towards learning.

Early intervention is also essential in the field of healthcare, particularly in addressing developmental delays, disabilities, and mental health issues in children. For example, early intervention programs for children with autism spectrum disorders have been shown to be highly effective in improving communication skills, social interactions, and adaptive behaviors. By starting interventions early, healthcare professionals can maximize the impact of treatments and support children in achieving better long-term outcomes.

In the realm of social services, early intervention is critical in addressing risk factors and providing support to individuals and families facing challenges such as poverty, abuse, and neglect. By identifying and addressing these issues early on, social workers can help prevent more serious problems from arising and support individuals in building resilience and improving their well-being. For example, early intervention programs for at-risk families have been shown to reduce instances of child abuse and neglect, improve family functioning, and enhance child development outcomes. By providing support and resources early, social services can help create a more stable and supportive environment for individuals and families. By taking proactive and timely measures to address challenges and risks, professionals can help individuals develop necessary skills, overcome obstacles, and reach their full potential. Research consistently demonstrates the effectiveness of early intervention in improving outcomes in education, healthcare, and social services. By investing in early intervention programs and services, we can create a more equitable and supportive society where all individuals have the opportunity to thrive and succeed.

- Importance of early detection

The importance of early detection cannot be overstated when it comes to many aspects of our health and well-being. Early detection refers to the ability to identify a condition or disease in its earliest stages, before symptoms may be noticeable or before the disease has progressed to a more advanced stage. This early identification can be crucial in preventing or delaying the progression of a disease, improving treatment outcomes, and ultimately saving lives.

One of the key reasons why early detection is so important is that many diseases are much easier to treat when they are caught early. For example, cancer is often much more responsive to treatment when it is detected in its early stages. In some cases, early detection can even lead to a complete cure. On the other hand, if cancer is not detected until it has progressed to a more advanced stage, treatment may be much more difficult and the chances of a successful outcome may be lower.

Early detection can also help to prevent the spread of certain diseases. For diseases that are contagious, such as influenza or tuberculosis, early detection can help to identify cases before they have a chance to spread to others. This can be especially important in preventing outbreaks of infectious diseases in communities or even on a larger scale.

In addition to its impact on individual health, early detection can also have broader societal implications. For example, early detection of certain conditions may lead to decreased healthcare costs, as treating a disease in its early stages is often less expensive than treating it once it has progressed. Early detection can also help to reduce the burden on healthcare systems by preventing the need for more intensive treatments or hospitalizations.

There are many ways in which early detection can be achieved. Screening programs, which involve testing large numbers of people for a particular condition, can be an effective way to identify cases early. For example, mammograms for breast cancer and colonoscopies for colon cancer are both types of screening tests that can help to detect these diseases in their early stages.

It is also important for individuals to be aware of the signs and symptoms of common diseases and to seek medical attention if they notice any unusual changes in their health. Regular check-ups with healthcare providers can also help to identify potential issues early on. In some cases, genetic testing may be recommended for individuals with a family history of certain diseases in order to detect any predispositions to these conditions. By identifying diseases in their earliest stages, we can improve treatment outcomes, prevent the spread of disease, and ultimately save lives. It is important for both individuals and healthcare systems to prioritize early detection in order to achieve the best possible health outcomes for all.

Chapter 3: Building a supportive environment for boys with dyslexia

- CREATING A SAFE AND empowering space for boys

Creating a safe and empowering space for boys is crucial in today's society, as they face a myriad of challenges and pressures that can impact their mental, emotional, and physical well-being. Boys are often socialized to suppress their emotions, conform to traditional masculine norms, and exhibit behavior that may not align with their true selves. This can lead to feelings of isolation, low self-esteem, and difficulties in forming meaningful relationships. By establishing a supportive environment that encourages boys to express themselves, explore their interests, and develop healthy communication skills, we can help them navigate these challenges and thrive in all aspects of their lives.

One key aspect of creating a safe and empowering space for boys is promoting open and honest communication. Boys are often taught to hide their emotions and tough it out, which can lead to a sense of isolation and loneliness. By encouraging boys to share their thoughts and feelings, we can help them build strong connections with others and develop a greater sense of self-awareness. This can be achieved through group discussions, mentorship programs, and one-on-one sessions with counselors or trusted adults. By providing a safe space where boys feel heard and understood, we can help them develop the skills they need to express themselves effectively and navigate their emotions in a healthy way.

In addition to promoting communication, creating a safe and empowering space for boys also involves challenging traditional gender norms and stereotypes. Boys are often taught to be strong, stoic, and independent, which can limit their ability to express vulnerability, seek help when needed, or explore interests that may not align with societal expectations. By challenging these norms and promoting a more inclusive and diverse view of masculinity, we can help boys develop a greater sense of self-acceptance and authenticity. This can be achieved by providing opportunities for boys to explore a wide range of interests and activities, regardless of whether they are traditionally considered "masculine" or "feminine. " By encouraging boys to be true to themselves and embrace their unique qualities, we can help them build confidence, resilience, and a strong sense of identity.

Another important aspect of creating a safe and empowering space for boys is addressing issues related to bullying, violence, and aggression. Boys are often socialized to compete with one another, assert dominance, and resolve conflicts through physical means. This can lead to harmful behaviors such as bullying, aggression, and violence, which can have lasting negative effects on both the perpetrator and the victim. By providing education on healthy conflict resolution, empathy, and respect for others, we can help boys develop the skills they need to navigate challenging situations in a constructive and non-violent way. This can be achieved through workshops, role-playing exercises, and peer mediation programs that teach boys how to communicate effectively, listen actively, and work together to find peaceful solutions. By promoting a culture of respect, empathy, and non-violence, we can help boys build healthy relationships, resolve conflicts peacefully, and contribute to a more harmonious and inclusive community. By promoting open and honest communication, challenging traditional gender norms, and addressing issues related to bullying and violence, we can help boys develop the skills they need to navigate the challenges they face and thrive in all aspects of their lives. Through education, support, and empowerment, we can create a world where boys feel valued, respected, and free to be themselves. It is up to all of us to come together, challenge the status quo, and create a better future for boys everywhere.

- Encouraging open communication and emotional expression

Open communication and emotional expression are crucial aspects of building strong relationships, both personally and professionally. It is essential to create a safe and supportive environment where individuals feel comfortable expressing their thoughts, feelings, and needs without fear of judgment or reprisal. By encouraging open communication and emotional expression, we can foster trust, understanding, and collaboration within our relationships.

One way to promote open communication and emotional expression is to actively listen to others. Listening involves not only hearing what someone is saying but also understanding the underlying emotions and motivations behind their words. By listening attentively and without judgment, we demonstrate empathy and create a space where individuals feel heard and understood. This can help build trust and strengthen relationships, as it shows that we value and respect the feelings and perspectives of others.

Another important aspect of encouraging open communication and emotional expression is creating a supportive and non-judgmental environment. It is essential to create a culture where individuals feel safe sharing their thoughts, feelings, and vulnerabilities without fear of criticism or rejection. This can be achieved by practicing empathy, compassion, and understanding towards others, as well as fostering a culture of respect and acceptance within our relationships. By creating a safe and supportive environment, we can encourage individuals to be more open and vulnerable in their communication, leading to deeper connections and more meaningful relationships.

In addition to creating a safe and supportive environment, it is important to actively encourage and validate the emotional expression of others. Emotions are a natural and important part of the human experience, and it is essential to acknowledge and validate the feelings of others, even if we may not always understand or agree with them. By validating the emotions of others, we show that we respect and accept their feelings, which can help build trust and strengthen our relationships. Validating emotions can also help individuals feel heard and understood, leading to more open and honest communication.

It is also important to practice self-awareness and emotional intelligence when encouraging open communication and emotional expression. By understanding our own emotions and motivations, we can better empathize with others and create a space where individuals feel comfortable sharing their feelings and thoughts. Self-awareness can help us recognize our own biases, judgments, and assumptions, allowing us to approach communication with an open mind and a willingness to learn from others. Emotional intelligence involves recognizing and managing our own emotions, as well as understanding and empathizing with the emotions of others. By practicing self-awareness and emotional intelligence, we can create a more authentic and meaningful connection with others, leading to deeper and more fulfilling relationships. By actively listening, creating a supportive environment, validating emotions, and practicing self-awareness and emotional intelligence, we can create a culture of trust, understanding, and collaboration within our relationships. By fostering open communication and emotional expression, we can build deeper connections with others, leading to more fulfilling and authentic relationships in both our personal and professional lives.

- Fostering a positive self-image

Fostering a positive self-image is crucial for leading a happy and fulfilling life. Having a positive self-image means having a healthy and realistic view of oneself, feeling confident in one's abilities and worth, and being able to see the good qualities in oneself. It is important because a positive self-image can lead to better mental health, higher self-esteem, stronger relationships, and overall improved well-being. However, building and maintaining a positive self-image is not always easy, as we live in a society that often promotes unrealistic standards and fosters negative self-talk. Therefore, it is important to deliberately work on cultivating a positive self-image through self-awareness, self-care, and self-compassion.

One way to foster a positive self-image is by practicing self-awareness. This involves being mindful of our thoughts, feelings, and behaviors, and understanding how they influence our self-image. By being aware of our inner dialogue, we can identify negative self-talk and replace it with positive affirmations. For example, instead of saying "I'm not good enough" or "I'm a failure," we can reframe these thoughts to say "I am capable and worthy" or "I am learning and growing. " Self-awareness also involves acknowledging our strengths and accomplishments, and celebrating them. This can help boost our self-esteem and confidence, and remind us of our inherent worthiness.

Another important aspect of fostering a positive self-image is practicing self-care. This means taking care of our physical, emotional, and mental well-being, and treating ourselves with kindness and compassion. Self-care can include engaging in activities that bring us joy and relaxation, such as exercise, meditation, hobbies, or spending time with loved ones. It can also involve setting boundaries with others, saying no when necessary, and prioritizing our own needs and wants. By practicing self-care, we can build resilience, reduce stress, and improve our overall sense of self-worth. This, in turn, can help us maintain a positive self-image and navigate life's challenges with grace and confidence.

Furthermore, fostering a positive self-image involves practicing self-compassion. Self-compassion is the act of treating ourselves with kindness, understanding, and acceptance, especially in times of struggle or failure. Instead of being self-critical or judgmental, self-compassion involves offering ourselves comfort, support, and encouragement. Research has shown that self-compassion is linked to greater emotional well-being, resilience, and overall life satisfaction. By being kind to ourselves and treating ourselves with the same care and compassion we would offer to a friend, we can cultivate a positive self-image and develop a healthy relationship with ourselves. By practicing self-awareness, self-care, and self-compassion, we can build a healthy and realistic view of ourselves, cultivate self-esteem and confidence, and improve our overall well-being. While it may take time and effort to develop a positive self-image, the benefits are well worth it. So, let us strive to be kind to ourselves, acknowledge our strengths and accomplishments, and treat ourselves with the love and respect we deserve. By doing so, we can foster a positive self-image and live a more joyful and authentic life.

Chapter 4: Developing coping strategies for daily challenges

- TEACHING PROBLEM-SOLVING skills

Problem-solving skills are an essential component of a well-rounded education. These skills are not only valuable in academic settings but are also crucial in the workplace and in everyday life. Teaching problem-solving skills is therefore a vital part of the educational process, as it equips students with the ability to think critically, analyze situations, and come up with creative solutions. In this essay, we will discuss the importance of teaching problem-solving skills, as well as strategies and approaches that educators can use to help students develop these skills.

One of the key reasons why problem-solving skills are so important is that they enable individuals to navigate the complexities of a rapidly changing world. In today's fast-paced society, being able to solve problems efficiently and effectively is a valuable asset. Whether it's in the workplace, where employees are often required to think on their feet and come up with innovative solutions to unexpected challenges, or in personal life, where individuals are faced with a myriad of everyday problems to solve, the ability to problem-solve is essential.

Furthermore, problem-solving skills are closely linked to critical thinking skills. By teaching students how to analyze situations, identify underlying issues, and come up with creative solutions, educators are helping them develop their critical thinking abilities. Critical thinking is the ability to evaluate information, arguments, and evidence in a logical and systematic way. It involves being able to recognize biases and assumptions, evaluate the validity of arguments, and draw thoughtful conclusions. By teaching problem-solving skills, educators are effectively teaching students how to think critically, which is a vital skill in today's information-rich society.

So how can educators effectively teach problem-solving skills to students. One approach is to provide students with opportunities to practice and develop their problem-solving skills in a variety of contexts. For example, educators can incorporate problem-solving activities into lessons, such as group projects, case studies, and real-world scenarios. These activities can help students apply their knowledge and skills to real-world problems, thereby enhancing their problem-solving abilities.

Another approach is to teach students specific problem-solving strategies and techniques. For example, educators can introduce students to the concept of "design thinking," a problem-solving approach that involves empathizing with users, defining the problem, ideating potential solutions, prototyping and testing those solutions, and iterating based on feedback. By teaching students these specific strategies, educators can provide them with a framework for approaching and solving problems in a systematic way.

In addition, educators can also encourage students to develop their creativity and innovation skills. Problem-solving often requires thinking outside the box and coming up with novel solutions to complex problems. By fostering creativity and innovation in the classroom, educators can help students develop the mindset and skills necessary to tackle difficult challenges and come up with innovative solutions. By equipping students with the ability to think critically, analyze situations, and come up with creative solutions, educators are preparing them for success in a fast-paced and complex world. By providing students with opportunities to practice and develop their problem-solving skills, teaching them specific problem-solving strategies and techniques, and fostering creativity and innovation, educators can help students become effective problem-solvers who are well-equipped to tackle challenges in any area of life.

- Encouraging self-advocacy

Encouraging self-advocacy is an essential aspect of personal development and empowerment. Self-advocacy refers to the ability to speak up for oneself, express one's needs and preferences, and assert one's rights in various situations. It is a crucial skill that can help individuals navigate complex social systems, assert their autonomy, and advocate for their own well-being.

One of the key benefits of self-advocacy is that it empowers individuals to take control of their own lives and make informed decisions. By advocating for oneself, individuals can ensure that their needs and rights are met, rather than relying on others to do so for them. This can be particularly important in situations where individuals may be vulnerable or marginalized, such as in healthcare settings or educational environments.

Self-advocacy also plays a critical role in fostering independence and self-reliance. When individuals are able to advocate for themselves effectively, they are less likely to rely on others to make decisions on their behalf. This can help to build self-confidence and a sense of autonomy, as individuals learn to trust their own judgment and abilities.

Moreover, self-advocacy can lead to improved communication and interpersonal skills. By learning how to express oneself clearly and assertively, individuals can enhance their ability to navigate social interactions and relationships. This can be particularly beneficial in professional settings, where effective communication is key to success.

In order to encourage self-advocacy, it is important to provide individuals with the tools and resources they need to develop this skill. This may involve teaching individuals how to identify their own needs and preferences, assert their rights in various situations, and communicate effectively with others. It may also involve creating a supportive and empowering environment in which individuals feel comfortable speaking up for themselves.

One way to promote self-advocacy is to provide individuals with opportunities to practice and develop this skill in a safe and supportive environment. This could involve role-playing exercises, group discussions, or scenarios that simulate real-life situations in which self-advocacy is needed. By practicing these skills in a controlled setting, individuals can build their confidence and competence in advocating for themselves.

Additionally, it is important to foster a culture of respect and empowerment in which individuals feel valued and encouraged to speak up for themselves. This may involve promoting a sense of agency and autonomy, and encouraging individuals to take an active role in decision-making processes that affect them. By creating a supportive and inclusive environment, individuals are more likely to feel empowered to advocate for themselves and assert their rights. By encouraging self-advocacy through education, practice, and creating a supportive environment, individuals can develop the confidence and competence they need to navigate complex social systems and advocate for themselves effectively. Ultimately, self-advocacy is an essential aspect of personal development and empowerment that can lead to greater independence, self-reliance, and improved communication skills.

- Building emotional intelligence

Emotional intelligence (EI) has gained increasing recognition in recent years as a crucial skill for success in both personal and professional domains. While traditional intelligence (IQ) may measure one's cognitive abilities, emotional intelligence encompasses the ability to understand, manage, and express one's own emotions, as well as to recognize and empathize with the emotions of others. This set of skills plays a significant role in forming and maintaining healthy relationships, making sound decisions, and effectively managing stress and conflicts. In this paper, we will explore the importance of building emotional intelligence, the key components of EI, and strategies for enhancing these skills in order to thrive in various aspects of life.

One of the key reasons why emotional intelligence is essential is its impact on interpersonal relationships. Individuals with high EI are better equipped to navigate social interactions and communicate effectively with others. They are able to understand the emotions and needs of those around them, which fosters trust, empathy, and collaboration. This, in turn, leads to stronger relationships and more positive outcomes in both personal and professional settings. Research has shown that individuals with high emotional intelligence have higher levels of job satisfaction, better teamwork skills, and are more likely to be promoted in the workplace.

Another important aspect of emotional intelligence is its role in decision-making. Emotions play a significant role in the choices we make, and individuals with high EI are better able to regulate their emotions and make decisions that are rational and objective. By being aware of their own feelings and how they may affect their choices, individuals can avoid impulsive decision-making and consider the long-term consequences of their actions. This ability to think critically and make informed decisions is a key characteristic of emotionally intelligent individuals.

Managing stress and conflicts is yet another important aspect of emotional intelligence. In today's fast-paced and interconnected world, the ability to remain calm under pressure and resolve conflicts peacefully is invaluable. Individuals with high EI have developed coping mechanisms that allow them to effectively deal with stress and diffuse tense situations. By understanding their own emotions and those of others, they are better able to communicate assertively, listen actively, and find solutions that are mutually beneficial. This skill set not only leads to healthier relationships but also contributes to a more positive work environment and improved overall well-being.

So, how can one go about building emotional intelligence. One of the first steps is to develop self-awareness. This involves recognizing one's own emotions, strengths, and weaknesses, and understanding how these factors influence one's thoughts and behaviors. Journaling, meditation, and seeking feedback from others can all be effective ways to enhance self-awareness. Another important component of emotional intelligence is self-regulation, or the ability to control one's emotions and impulses. This can be developed through practices such as mindfulness, deep breathing, and cognitive reappraisal, which involves reframing negative thoughts in a more positive light.

Empathy is another key aspect of emotional intelligence, as it involves understanding and sharing the feelings of others. By actively listening, showing compassion, and considering the perspectives of others, individuals can cultivate empathy and build stronger connections with those around them. Social skills are also important in developing emotional intelligence, as they involve effectively communicating, negotiating, and resolving conflicts with others. Practicing active listening, assertiveness, and collaboration can all help improve social skills and enhance emotional intelligence. By developing self-awareness, self-regulation, empathy, and social skills, individuals can enhance their emotional intelligence and improve their relationships, decision-making, and overall well-being. Building emotional intelligence is an ongoing process that requires self-reflection, practice, and a willingness to learn and grow. By prioritizing emotional intelligence, individuals can unlock their full potential and thrive in all aspects of life.

Chapter 5: Navigating the education system

- UNDERSTANDING THE special education process

Special education is a field of education that focuses on providing tailored instruction and support to students with disabilities. The goal of special education is to ensure that all students have access to a high-quality education and are given the tools and resources they need to succeed academically and socially. The special education process is a complex and multifaceted system that involves a variety of steps and stakeholders, including parents, teachers, administrators, and special education professionals.

The special education process begins with the identification and evaluation of students who may be in need of special education services. This process is typically initiated when a student is struggling academically or behaviorally and interventions put in place by general education teachers are not effective. Parents or teachers may request an evaluation, or school personnel may identify a student who may be in need of special education services through observation or assessment data.

Once a student is identified as potentially needing special education services, a comprehensive evaluation is conducted to determine the student's strengths and weaknesses, as well as any disabilities or challenges that may be impacting their academic performance. This evaluation may include assessments in areas such as cognitive abilities, academic achievement, social and emotional functioning, and speech and language development. The evaluation team may also gather information from parents, teachers, and other professionals who have worked with the student.

Based on the results of the evaluation, an Individualized Education Program (IEP) is developed for the student. An IEP is a legal document that outlines the student's unique needs and the special education and related services that will be provided to address those needs. The IEP is developed by a team of individuals, including the student's parents, teachers, special education professionals, and administrators. The IEP includes information such as the student's present levels of academic achievement and functional performance, annual goals and objectives, special education and related services to be provided, accommodations and modifications, and progress monitoring.

Once the IEP is developed, it must be implemented by the student's teachers and service providers. This may involve modifications to the student's curriculum, instruction, or learning environment to accommodate their individual needs. It is important for teachers to collaborate with one another and communicate regularly with parents to ensure that the student's needs are being met and that progress is being made towards their goals.

Progress monitoring is a critical component of the special education process. Teachers and service providers must collect data on the student's progress towards their IEP goals and objectives, and use this information to make informed decisions about the student's educational program. Progress monitoring may involve regular assessments, observations, and data collection, as well as ongoing communication with parents and other team members.

Throughout the special education process, it is essential for all stakeholders to work together collaboratively to support the student's academic and social-emotional development. This may involve regular team meetings, communication between parents and teachers, and coordination of services and supports. Collaboration and communication are key to ensuring that all students receive the individualized support they need to be successful in school and beyond. By understanding the special education process and the roles and responsibilities of all team members, we can ensure that all students have access to a high-quality education and the tools and resources they need to succeed. Through collaboration, communication, and a commitment to meeting the individual needs of each student, we can create an inclusive and supportive educational environment that promotes learning and growth for all.

- **Advocating for accommodations and supports**

Advocating for accommodations and supports is a crucial aspect of ensuring that individuals with disabilities have equal access to opportunities and are able to fully participate in society. Accommodations and supports can play a significant role in leveling the playing field for individuals with disabilities, helping them to overcome barriers and reach their full potential. In many cases, accommodations and supports are necessary to ensure that individuals with disabilities are able to access educational, employment, and other opportunities on an equal basis with their non-disabled peers.

One important aspect of advocating for accommodations and supports is understanding the legal framework that governs the rights of individuals with disabilities. In many countries, including the United States, Canada, and the European Union, laws have been put in place to protect the rights of individuals with disabilities and to ensure that they have access to the accommodations and supports they need to participate fully in society. These laws, such as the Americans with Disabilities Act (ADA) in the United States, the Canadian Charter of Rights and Freedoms in Canada, and the European Union Directive on the rights of persons with disabilities in the European Union, provide a framework for advocating for accommodations and supports and can be a powerful tool in ensuring that individuals with disabilities are able to access the accommodations and supports they need.

Another important aspect of advocating for accommodations and supports is understanding the types of accommodations and supports that may be available to individuals with disabilities. Accommodations can take many forms, depending on the individual's needs and the specific barriers they face. For example, accommodations in the workplace may include flexible hours, modified job duties, or assistive technology, while accommodations in education may include extended time on exams, note-taking services, or access to a sign language interpreter. Supports, on the other hand, may include services such as counseling, mentoring, or coaching to help individuals with disabilities navigate challenges and reach their goals.

Advocating for accommodations and supports may involve working with a variety of stakeholders, including employers, educators, service providers, and policy makers. It is important to build strong partnerships with these stakeholders to ensure that individuals with disabilities are able to access the accommodations and supports they need. This may involve providing education and training on the rights of individuals with disabilities, advocating for policy changes to improve access to accommodations and supports, and working to build inclusive environments that prioritize equity and accessibility for all.

One key aspect of advocating for accommodations and supports is understanding the individual needs of individuals with disabilities and working to tailor accommodations and supports to meet those needs. Every individual is unique, and what works for one person may not work for another. It is important to listen to the individual with a disability and involve them in the decision-making process when identifying accommodations and supports. This collaborative approach can help ensure that the accommodations and supports are effective in meeting the individual's needs and empowering them to succeed. By understanding the legal framework that governs the rights of individuals with disabilities, identifying the types of accommodations and supports that may be available, working with stakeholders to build partnerships, and tailoring accommodations and supports to meet individual needs, advocates can help individuals with disabilities overcome barriers and reach their full potential. Advocating for accommodations and supports is a powerful tool in promoting equality, inclusion, and diversity in our communities and society as a whole.

- Building partnerships with teachers and school staff

Building partnerships with teachers and school staff is crucial for the success of any educational institution. These partnerships can lead to improved communication, collaboration, and support for all stakeholders involved in the learning process. By fostering strong relationships with teachers and staff, school leaders can create a positive and productive work environment that benefits both students and educators.

One key aspect of building partnerships with teachers and school staff is establishing open lines of communication. School leaders should make an effort to regularly communicate with teachers and staff to keep them informed about important updates, decisions, and initiatives. This can be done through staff meetings, emails, newsletters, or one-on-one conversations. By keeping everyone in the loop, school leaders can ensure that all members of the school community are on the same page and working towards common goals.

Another important strategy for building partnerships with teachers and school staff is fostering a culture of collaboration. School leaders should encourage teachers and staff to work together to share ideas, resources, and best practices. Collaborative planning and problem-solving can lead to more effective teaching strategies and a more cohesive learning environment for students. By promoting teamwork and collaboration among educators, school leaders can create a more supportive and enriching work environment for all.

In addition to communication and collaboration, building partnerships with teachers and school staff also involves providing support and professional development opportunities. School leaders should invest in ongoing training and development for teachers and staff to help them grow and improve as educators. By offering workshops, seminars, and other learning opportunities, school leaders can empower teachers and staff to enhance their skills and stay up-to-date on the latest educational trends and research. This investment in professional development can help teachers and staff feel valued and supported, leading to increased job satisfaction and retention.

Furthermore, building partnerships with teachers and school staff requires a commitment to fostering a positive school culture. School leaders should create a welcoming and inclusive environment where all members of the school community feel respected and supported. This can be achieved through promoting diversity and equity, recognizing and celebrating the contributions of teachers and staff, and addressing any issues of bias or discrimination that may arise. By creating a positive school culture, school leaders can build trust and rapport with teachers and staff, leading to stronger partnerships and a more harmonious work environment. By prioritizing communication, collaboration, support, and a positive school culture, school leaders can establish strong relationships with teachers and staff that benefit everyone involved in the learning process. Through these partnerships, educators can work together to improve student outcomes, create a more engaging and supportive learning environment, and ultimately help all students succeed.

Chapter 6: Empowering boys to advocate for themselves

- TEACHING SELF-ADVOCACY skills

Teaching self-advocacy skills is a crucial aspect of education that empowers students to take control of their own learning and development. Self-advocacy involves being able to communicate one's own needs, interests, and preferences to others, as well as being able to make informed decisions and take responsibility for one's own actions. By teaching students these skills, educators can help them become more independent, confident, and successful in navigating the challenges they face both inside and outside of the classroom.

One key aspect of teaching self-advocacy skills is promoting self-awareness in students. This involves helping students understand their strengths, weaknesses, and learning preferences, as well as their own goals and aspirations. By helping students develop a clear sense of self, educators can empower them to advocate for themselves effectively and confidently. This can involve activities such as self-assessment exercises, goal-setting tasks, and reflective journaling, which can help students identify their own needs and priorities.

Another important aspect of teaching self-advocacy skills is developing students' communication skills. Effective self-advocacy relies on being able to communicate one's needs clearly and assertively, whether that be to peers, teachers, or other adults. Educators can help students build these skills through activities such as role-playing exercises, group discussions, and public speaking tasks. By providing students with opportunities to practice their communication skills in a safe and supportive environment, educators can help them develop the confidence and assertiveness needed to advocate for themselves effectively in real-life situations.

In addition to promoting self-awareness and communication skills, teaching self-advocacy skills also involves helping students develop problem-solving and decision-making abilities. Self-advocacy often requires students to navigate complex social and academic situations, and being able to think critically and make informed choices is essential for success. Educators can help students build these skills by engaging them in activities that promote critical thinking, creative problem-solving, and ethical decision-making. By developing these skills, educators can empower students to advocate for themselves in a thoughtful and responsible manner.

Furthermore, teaching self-advocacy skills involves fostering a supportive and inclusive learning environment that encourages students to speak up and take initiative. Educators can create such an environment by building trust and rapport with students, listening to their concerns and feedback, and validating their experiences and perspectives. By showing students that their voices are valued and respected, educators can help them feel more comfortable and confident in advocating for themselves. This can also involve promoting a culture of mutual respect and collaboration among students, so that they feel supported in their efforts to speak up and assert their needs.

Ultimately, teaching self-advocacy skills is a valuable investment in the future success and well-being of students. By empowering students to take ownership of their own learning and development, educators can help them build the confidence, independence, and resilience needed to thrive in an increasingly complex and competitive world. By promoting self-awareness, communication skills, problem-solving abilities, and a supportive learning environment, educators can equip students with the tools they need to advocate for themselves effectively and achieve their full potential. It is essential for educators to prioritize teaching self-advocacy skills in their classrooms, as it is a fundamental aspect of promoting student success and well-being.

- Building confidence and self-esteem

Building confidence and self-esteem are crucial aspects of personal development that can significantly impact various areas of an individual's life. Confidence refers to a belief in one's abilities and judgment, while self-esteem involves how one values themselves and their self-worth. Both confidence and self-esteem play a crucial role in how we perceive ourselves, interact with others, and navigate challenges in life. While some individuals may naturally possess high levels of confidence and self-esteem, others may struggle in these areas and require intentional effort to cultivate them.

One key factor in building confidence and self-esteem is recognizing and challenging negative self-talk and limiting beliefs. Negative self-talk involves thoughts or beliefs that undermine our confidence and self-esteem, such as "I'm not good enough" or "I can't do this. " These negative beliefs can be deeply ingrained and may stem from past experiences, societal influences, or comparisons to others. By identifying and challenging these negative thoughts, individuals can begin to reframe their thinking and develop a more positive and empowering mindset.

Another essential aspect of building confidence and self-esteem is setting and achieving goals. Setting realistic and achievable goals can help individuals build confidence as they see themselves making progress and accomplishing tasks. By breaking down larger goals into smaller, more manageable steps, individuals can build momentum and gain a sense of achievement that boosts their self-esteem. Celebrating even small victories along the way can further reinforce positive feelings of confidence and self-worth.

Additionally, building confidence and self-esteem can be supported by cultivating a growth mindset. A growth mindset involves believing that one's abilities and intelligence can be developed through effort and perseverance. This mindset encourages individuals to view challenges as opportunities for growth and learning, rather than as threats to their self-esteem. By approaching challenges with a growth mindset, individuals can build resilience and confidence in their ability to overcome obstacles and achieve their goals.

Practicing self-care and self-compassion are also essential components of building confidence and self-esteem. Taking care of oneself physically, emotionally, and mentally can help individuals feel more confident and secure in themselves. This can involve getting enough rest, eating well, exercising regularly, and engaging in activities that bring joy and fulfillment. Additionally, practicing self-compassion involves being kind and understanding towards oneself, especially in times of struggle or failure. By treating oneself with the same kindness and compassion as one would a friend, individuals can boost their self-esteem and build a stronger sense of self-worth.

Furthermore, developing a support network of friends, family, or mentors can also contribute to building confidence and self-esteem. Surrounding oneself with positive and supportive individuals who believe in one's abilities can provide encouragement and validation. Building strong connections with others can help individuals feel more connected, valued, and accepted, which can in turn boost their confidence and self-esteem. Seeking out mentors or role models who exemplify qualities one aspires to can also provide guidance and inspiration in developing confidence and self-esteem. By recognizing and challenging negative self-talk, setting and achieving goals, cultivating a growth mindset, practicing self-care and self-compassion, and developing a support network, individuals can build confidence and self-esteem. These qualities are essential for navigating life's challenges, pursuing goals, and fostering positive relationships with oneself and others. By investing in one's personal development and actively working towards building confidence and self-esteem, individuals can lead more fulfilling and empowered lives.

- Encouraging independence

Encouraging independence in individuals is a key component of fostering personal growth and development. Independence is the ability to think and act for oneself, making decisions and taking responsibility for one's actions. It is an important skill to cultivate in individuals of all ages, as it enables them to navigate the challenges of life with confidence and resilience. By encouraging independence, we empower individuals to become self-reliant and to lead fulfilling and meaningful lives.

One of the fundamental ways to encourage independence is to provide individuals with opportunities to make choices and decisions for themselves. This could involve giving them the freedom to choose their own activities, set their own goals, and solve their own problems. By allowing individuals to make decisions, we empower them to take ownership of their lives and to learn from their experiences. This process of trial and error is essential for personal growth and development, as it helps individuals to develop their problem-solving skills and decision-making abilities.

In addition to providing opportunities for individuals to make choices and decisions, it is also important to support them in learning new skills and taking on new challenges. Building independence is a gradual process that requires individuals to step out of their comfort zones and try new things. By encouraging individuals to push themselves beyond their limits, we help them to develop the confidence and resilience needed to face life's challenges. This might involve providing individuals with the resources and support they need to learn new skills, such as enrolling in a training program or seeking out a mentor to guide them through the learning process.

Furthermore, it is essential to foster a sense of responsibility and accountability in individuals in order to encourage independence. Responsibility is the willingness to take ownership of one's actions and the consequences that result from them. By instilling a sense of responsibility in individuals, we help them to understand the impact of their choices and actions on themselves and others. This awareness is a key aspect of independence, as it empowers individuals to make informed decisions and to take responsibility for the outcomes of their choices.

Another important aspect of encouraging independence is to provide individuals with the support and guidance they need to overcome obstacles and challenges. Independence does not mean going it alone – it is about knowing when to ask for help and how to leverage the resources available to overcome difficulties. By providing individuals with a support network of friends, family, mentors, and professionals, we empower them to navigate the ups and downs of life with confidence and resilience. This support network can offer advice, encouragement, and practical assistance to help individuals overcome obstacles and achieve their goals. By providing individuals with opportunities to make choices and decisions, support in learning new skills, fostering a sense of responsibility and accountability, and providing a support network to help them overcome challenges, we empower them to lead fulfilling and meaningful lives. Independence is not about going it alone, but about knowing when to ask for help and how to leverage the resources available to overcome obstacles. By fostering independence in individuals, we enable them to become self-reliant and resilient individuals who can navigate life's challenges with confidence and grace.

Chapter 7: Building social connections and support networks

- HELPING BOYS CULTIVATE meaningful relationships

Helping boys cultivate meaningful relationships is an important aspect of their overall social and emotional development. Boys, like all individuals, benefit from having strong connections with others - whether it be with family members, friends, or romantic partners. However, societal norms and expectations often hinder boys from building and maintaining these relationships in a healthy and fulfilling way. This can have negative consequences in their later lives, impacting their mental health, self-esteem, and overall well-being. Therefore, it is crucial to provide boys with the tools and support they need to cultivate meaningful relationships from a young age.

One of the key factors in helping boys cultivate meaningful relationships is teaching them effective communication skills. Boys are often socialized to be stoic and suppress their emotions, which can hinder their ability to express themselves openly and honestly in relationships. By teaching boys how to communicate their thoughts and feelings in a healthy and respectful manner, we can help them build stronger connections with others. This includes teaching boys how to listen actively, empathize with others, and express their own emotions in a constructive way. By fostering open and honest communication, we can help boys develop deeper and more meaningful relationships with those around them.

Another important aspect of helping boys cultivate meaningful relationships is teaching them about boundaries and consent. Boys need to understand the importance of respecting others' boundaries and seeking consent in all of their interactions. By teaching boys the importance of consent and boundaries, we can help them develop respectful and healthy relationships with others. This includes teaching boys how to recognize and respect others' boundaries, as well as how to communicate their own boundaries in a clear and assertive manner. By fostering a culture of respect and consent, we can help boys build relationships based on mutual trust and understanding.

In addition to communication skills and understanding boundaries, it is also important to encourage boys to develop empathy and emotional intelligence. Boys are often taught to prioritize rationality and logic over emotions, which can hinder their ability to empathize with others and understand their emotional needs. By helping boys develop their emotional intelligence, we can help them cultivate more meaningful and fulfilling relationships. This includes teaching boys how to recognize and manage their own emotions, as well as how to empathize with others and respond to their emotional needs. By fostering empathy and emotional intelligence, we can help boys build deeper connections with others and navigate their relationships more effectively.

Furthermore, it is important to challenge traditional gender stereotypes and expectations that hinder boys from cultivating meaningful relationships. Society often teaches boys to be aggressive, dominant, and emotionally distant, which can limit their ability to form authentic and fulfilling connections with others. By challenging these stereotypes and encouraging boys to express a wider range of emotions and behaviors, we can help them develop more authentic and meaningful relationships. This includes challenging societal norms that equate masculinity with emotional detachment and encouraging boys to embrace vulnerability and empathy in their relationships. By challenging these stereotypes and expectations, we can help boys develop healthier and more fulfilling relationships with others. By teaching boys effective communication skills, boundaries and consent, empathy and emotional intelligence, and challenging traditional gender stereotypes, we can help boys build stronger and more fulfilling relationships with others. It is important to provide boys with the tools and support they need to navigate their relationships in a healthy and respectful way. By fostering open and honest communication, empathy, and respect, we can help boys develop deeper connections with others and lead happier and more fulfilling lives.

- **Providing opportunities for social interaction**

Social interaction is an essential aspect of human life, impacting our mental, emotional, and physical well-being. It has been shown to reduce feelings of loneliness, improve mood, and enhance overall quality of life. Therefore, providing opportunities for social interaction is crucial in fostering a sense of connection and community among individuals. In this discussion, we will explore the importance of social interaction, how it can be facilitated, and the benefits it offers to individuals of all ages.

One of the key benefits of social interaction is its ability to combat feelings of loneliness and isolation. Research has shown that individuals who engage in regular social interactions tend to have lower levels of depression and anxiety. By providing opportunities for social interaction, we can create a support system for individuals who may be struggling with mental health issues or feeling disconnected from others. Whether it be through community events, support groups, or social clubs, fostering a sense of belonging and camaraderie is essential in promoting overall wellness.

Additionally, social interaction plays a role in improving mood and emotional well-being. When we engage with others in meaningful conversations or activities, our brains release chemicals like oxytocin and serotonin, which are known for boosting happiness and reducing stress levels. By creating spaces for individuals to connect and share experiences, we can create a positive and uplifting environment that promotes emotional resilience and mental wellness. This is particularly important in times of hardship or crisis, as social support can serve as a crucial lifeline for those in need.

Furthermore, social interaction has been linked to improved physical health outcomes. Studies have shown that individuals who have strong social connections tend to have better overall health and lower rates of chronic illnesses. By providing opportunities for social interaction, we can help individuals establish healthy habits, such as regular exercise, nutritious eating, and stress management techniques. Additionally, social interactions can serve as a form of accountability and motivation for individuals to prioritize their health and well-being. This holistic approach to wellness not only benefits individuals on a personal level but also contributes to the overall health of the community.

In order to provide opportunities for social interaction, it is important to create inclusive and welcoming spaces where individuals feel comfortable and engaged. This can be achieved through a variety of means, such as hosting community events, offering social clubs or groups, and providing resources for networking and support. By fostering open communication and collaboration, we can encourage individuals to connect with one another and build meaningful relationships. Additionally, incorporating technology and digital platforms can help bridge the gap for individuals who may have physical limitations or live in remote areas, allowing them to participate in social interactions virtually.

Moreover, it is important to recognize the diverse needs and preferences of individuals when providing opportunities for social interaction. Not everyone may feel comfortable in large social settings or group settings, so offering a range of options, from one-on-one interactions to larger gatherings, can help cater to different personalities and comfort levels. Additionally, considering cultural sensitivities and accessibility barriers is essential in ensuring that social opportunities are inclusive and accessible to all members of the community. By embracing diversity and individuality, we can create a rich tapestry of social connections that benefit everyone involved. By creating inclusive and welcoming spaces, promoting emotional resilience, and supporting physical health outcomes, we can help individuals thrive and flourish in a supportive environment. Through collaboration, communication, and creativity, we can build a strong foundation of social connections that enrich our lives and enhance our overall quality of life. Let us continue to prioritize social interaction as a fundamental aspect of human flourishing and well-being.

- Building a strong support system

Building a strong support system is essential for success in both personal and professional endeavors. A strong support system can provide encouragement, guidance, and resources to help individuals overcome challenges and achieve their goals. Whether it be friends, family, mentors, or colleagues, having a network of people who believe in your abilities and are willing to help you along the way can make a significant difference in your journey towards success.

One of the key components of building a strong support system is surrounding yourself with positive and uplifting individuals. These are the people who will listen to your ideas, offer constructive feedback, and cheer you on as you navigate through the ups and downs of life. Positive relationships can provide a sense of belonging and connection, which can boost confidence and motivation. Additionally, positivity is contagious, so being around positive people can help you maintain a optimistic outlook, even when faced with challenges.

Another important aspect of building a strong support system is fostering open and honest communication with those around you. Being able to share your thoughts, feelings, and concerns with others can help you gain perspective, receive valuable advice, and find solutions to problems. Honest communication is also key in building trust and mutual respect within your support network. When you feel comfortable being vulnerable and transparent with those in your support system, it creates a space for deeper connections and stronger relationships to form.

In addition to positive relationships and open communication, building a strong support system also involves seeking out mentors and role models who can offer guidance and wisdom based on their own experiences. Mentors can provide valuable insights, advice, and encouragement as you navigate your own path towards success. By learning from the experiences of others, you can avoid common pitfalls, gain valuable skills and knowledge, and make informed decisions about your own goals and aspirations. Having a mentor who believes in your potential and is willing to invest their time and expertise in your growth can be a game-changer in your personal and professional development.

Furthermore, building a strong support system involves actively seeking out opportunities to connect with like-minded individuals who share your values, interests, and goals. These could be peers, colleagues, or members of professional organizations who can offer unique perspectives, new ideas, and potential collaborations. By surrounding yourself with individuals who are driven, ambitious, and passionate about similar pursuits, you can create a sense of community and camaraderie that can help propel you towards success. Building a network of like-minded individuals can also provide access to valuable resources, information, and opportunities that you may not have been able to access on your own. Surrounding yourself with positive, uplifting individuals, fostering open and honest communication, seeking out mentors and role models, and connecting with like-minded peers are all important steps in creating a support network that can help you overcome challenges, achieve your goals, and reach your full potential. By investing time and effort in building and nurturing these relationships, you can create a solid foundation of support that will guide you through life's journey and empower you to thrive in all aspects of your life.

Chapter 8: Promoting positive mental health and well-being

- RECOGNIZING THE IMPACT of dyslexia on mental health

Dyslexia is a common learning disability that affects the way a person processes language, particularly when it comes to reading and writing. It is estimated that dyslexia affects up to 20% of people in the United States alone, making it an incredibly prevalent condition. While dyslexia is often associated with difficulties in reading and writing, it is important to recognize that it can also have a significant impact on mental health.

One of the ways dyslexia can affect mental health is through the frustration and stress that can come from struggling to read and write. For someone with dyslexia, simple tasks like reading a book or writing an email can be extremely challenging and time-consuming. This can lead to feelings of inadequacy, low self-esteem, and anxiety. It can also make it difficult to keep up with school or work, which can further contribute to feelings of stress and overwhelm.

In addition to the challenges of reading and writing, dyslexia can also affect a person's ability to organize and manage their thoughts. This can make it difficult to communicate effectively, both verbally and in writing. It can also make it harder to process information, follow instructions, and keep track of tasks. These difficulties can lead to feelings of frustration, confusion, and even depression.

Another way dyslexia can impact mental health is through the social and emotional challenges that can come from having a learning disability. People with dyslexia may face stigma, discrimination, and bullying from others who do not understand their condition. This can lead to feelings of isolation, loneliness, and shame. It can also make it harder to form relationships and connect with others, which can further contribute to mental health issues.

It is important to recognize the impact of dyslexia on mental health so that people with this condition can get the support and resources they need. By understanding the challenges that dyslexia can present, we can work to create a more inclusive and supportive environment for individuals with this learning disability. This can include providing accommodations in school and work settings, promoting awareness and understanding of dyslexia, and offering resources for coping with the emotional and mental health challenges that can come from having this condition. By recognizing the challenges that dyslexia can present, we can work to create a more supportive and understanding environment for individuals with this condition. It is important to provide resources and accommodations for people with dyslexia so that they can thrive and reach their full potential. By raising awareness and promoting understanding of dyslexia, we can help to improve the mental health and well-being of those affected by this learning disability.

- Teaching coping strategies for managing stress and anxiety

Stress and anxiety are common experiences for many individuals, especially in today's fast-paced and demanding society. Whether it be due to work pressures, personal relationships, financial concerns, or other factors, it is important for individuals to have effective coping strategies in place to manage and alleviate these feelings. As a result, teaching coping strategies for managing stress and anxiety is a crucial skill that can greatly benefit individuals in both their personal and professional lives.

One of the key coping strategies for managing stress and anxiety is developing healthy lifestyle habits. This includes maintaining a balanced diet, engaging in regular physical activity, getting an adequate amount of sleep, and practicing relaxation techniques such as deep breathing or meditation. Research has shown that these lifestyle habits can have a significant impact on reducing stress and anxiety levels. For example, regular exercise has been found to increase the production of endorphins, which are chemicals in the brain that act as natural painkillers and mood elevators. Additionally, eating a balanced diet that includes fruits, vegetables, whole grains, and lean proteins can provide the body with the necessary nutrients to support optimal brain function and mental well-being.

Another important coping strategy for managing stress and anxiety is practicing mindfulness and staying present in the moment. Mindfulness involves paying attention to one's thoughts, feelings, and surroundings without judgment or attachment. By focusing on the present moment and letting go of worries about the past or future, individuals can reduce the impact of stress and anxiety on their mental and emotional well-being. Research has shown that mindfulness practices, such as meditation or yoga, can help individuals cultivate a greater sense of calm, clarity, and emotional resilience.

In addition to healthy lifestyle habits and mindfulness practices, cognitive-behavioral strategies can also be effective in managing stress and anxiety. Cognitive-behavioral therapy (CBT) is a type of psychotherapy that focuses on changing negative thought patterns and behaviors that contribute to stress and anxiety. By identifying and challenging irrational beliefs, individuals can learn to replace them with more balanced and realistic thoughts. This can help individuals develop healthier coping mechanisms and improve their ability to manage stressful situations. Research has shown that CBT can be highly effective in treating a variety of mental health conditions, including anxiety disorders, depression, and post-traumatic stress disorder.

Furthermore, social support plays a crucial role in managing stress and anxiety. Having a strong support network of family, friends, or colleagues can provide individuals with a sense of comfort, validation, and encouragement during difficult times. Connecting with others who understand and empathize with one's struggles can help individuals feel less isolated and alone in their experiences. Research has shown that social support can buffer the negative effects of stress and anxiety on mental health and well-being. Engaging in activities that foster social connection, such as joining a support group or participating in community events, can help individuals build and maintain strong relationships that can help them navigate life's challenges. By incorporating healthy lifestyle habits, mindfulness practices, cognitive-behavioral strategies, and social support into one's daily routine, individuals can learn to effectively manage and alleviate stress and anxiety symptoms. These coping strategies not only provide individuals with the tools to navigate difficult situations, but also empower them to cultivate a greater sense of self-awareness, emotional balance, and psychological strength. In doing so, individuals can enhance their capacity to cope with life's stressors and challenges, leading to greater overall satisfaction and fulfillment in their lives.

- Encouraging resilience and perseverance

Resilience and perseverance are essential traits for success in various aspects of life. Whether in academics, career, relationships, or personal goals, the ability to bounce back from setbacks and keep pushing forward is crucial. Encouraging resilience and perseverance can help individuals navigate challenges more effectively and come out stronger on the other side.

One way to foster resilience and perseverance is to cultivate a growth mindset. People with a growth mindset believe that their abilities can be developed through hard work, dedication, and perseverance. This belief empowers them to face challenges head-on and see setbacks as opportunities for growth and learning. By encouraging a growth mindset in ourselves and others, we can help build resilience and perseverance in the face of adversity.

Building a strong support system is another important factor in promoting resilience and perseverance. Having a network of friends, family, mentors, and colleagues who can provide emotional support, guidance, and encouragement can make a significant difference in how we navigate challenges. Surrounding ourselves with people who believe in us and our ability to overcome obstacles can boost our resilience and motivation to keep pushing forward.

Setting realistic goals and breaking them down into smaller, achievable steps is also key to fostering resilience and perseverance. By establishing clear objectives and creating a plan to work towards them, we can maintain focus and motivation even when faced with setbacks. Celebrating small victories along the way can also help boost morale and keep us motivated to keep moving forward.

Practicing self-care and stress management techniques is essential for building resilience and perseverance. Taking care of ourselves physically, emotionally, and mentally can help us better cope with challenges and bounce back from setbacks. Engaging in activities that promote relaxation, such as exercise, meditation, or spending time with loved ones, can help recharge our batteries and build mental toughness.

Learning from past experiences and reflecting on our successes and failures can also help build resilience and perseverance. By taking the time to analyze what worked and what didn't in previous situations, we can gain valuable insights that can inform our approach to future challenges. This self-reflection can help us identify our strengths and areas for improvement, enabling us to better prepare for obstacles that may come our way. By fostering a growth mindset, building a strong support system, setting realistic goals, practicing self-care, and learning from past experiences, we can cultivate the resilience and perseverance needed to overcome obstacles and achieve our goals. With determination, dedication, and a positive attitude, we can navigate challenges with confidence and come out stronger on the other side.

Chapter 9: Celebrating successes and milestones

- RECOGNIZING AND CELEBRATING achievements

Recognizing and celebrating achievements is a vital aspect of fostering motivation, engagement, and a positive work culture within any organization. Acknowledging the hard work and accomplishments of individuals not only boosts morale and satisfaction but also encourages others to strive for excellence. By publicly recognizing achievements, organizations can create a sense of purpose and pride among their employees, leading to increased productivity and loyalty.

One of the key benefits of recognizing and celebrating achievements is the reinforcement of desired behaviors and values within an organization. When employees see their efforts being acknowledged and rewarded, they are more likely to continue demonstrating those behaviors and embodying the core values of the company. This can help to create a culture of excellence and high performance, where individuals are motivated to go above and beyond in their roles.

In addition to reinforcing desired behaviors, recognizing and celebrating achievements can also improve employee engagement and job satisfaction. When employees feel valued and appreciated for their contributions, they are more likely to be engaged and committed to their work. This can lead to higher levels of job satisfaction and lower rates of turnover, as employees are more likely to feel connected to the organization and its mission.

Furthermore, recognizing and celebrating achievements can have a positive impact on team dynamics and collaboration within an organization. By publicly acknowledging the achievements of individuals, organizations can promote a sense of camaraderie and teamwork among employees. This can lead to increased collaboration, communication, and support among team members, as they work together towards common goals and celebrate each other's successes.

In order to effectively recognize and celebrate achievements, organizations should establish clear criteria and processes for acknowledging accomplishments. This can include setting specific goals and targets for employees to strive towards, as well as establishing a system for tracking and evaluating their progress. It is important for organizations to communicate these criteria and goals clearly to employees, so that they understand what is expected of them and how their achievements will be recognized.

Additionally, organizations should consider implementing formal recognition programs to celebrate achievements. This can include rewards and incentives for reaching specific milestones, as well as public recognition through awards ceremonies or internal communications. By establishing formal recognition programs, organizations can ensure that achievements are consistently acknowledged and celebrated, and that employees feel motivated to continue striving for excellence. By publicly acknowledging and rewarding the accomplishments of individuals, organizations can reinforce desired behaviors and values, improve employee engagement and job satisfaction, and promote teamwork and collaboration. It is essential for organizations to establish clear criteria and processes for recognizing achievements, as well as to implement formal recognition programs to celebrate success. Ultimately, by recognizing and celebrating achievements, organizations can create a culture of excellence and high performance that benefits both employees and the organization as a whole.

- Building a sense of accomplishment and pride

Building a sense of accomplishment and pride is essential for personal growth and well-being. Achieving goals and overcoming challenges can boost self-esteem and confidence, leading to a greater sense of worth and satisfaction. When individuals set realistic objectives and work towards them diligently, they are more likely to experience a sense of achievement that can be a powerful motivator for continued success. By recognizing and celebrating their accomplishments, individuals can cultivate a positive self-image and a sense of pride in their abilities and efforts.

One key aspect of building a sense of accomplishment and pride is setting clear and achievable goals. When individuals have a clear idea of what they want to achieve and a plan for how to get there, they are more likely to stay motivated and focused. Setting measurable objectives with specific deadlines can help individuals track their progress and stay on track. By breaking larger goals into smaller, manageable tasks, individuals can build momentum and confidence as they work towards their ultimate goal.

Another important aspect of building a sense of accomplishment and pride is facing and overcoming challenges. While it can be tempting to avoid difficult tasks or situations, confronting obstacles head-on can lead to greater personal growth and a stronger sense of accomplishment. When individuals push themselves outside of their comfort zone and challenge themselves to tackle difficult problems, they can build resilience and develop valuable skills that can benefit them in the long run. Overcoming obstacles can also provide individuals with a sense of satisfaction and pride in their ability to persevere and succeed in the face of adversity.

Recognizing and celebrating accomplishments is crucial for building a sense of pride and accomplishment. Individuals should take the time to acknowledge and appreciate their efforts, no matter how small they may seem. By celebrating even small wins and milestones, individuals can boost their confidence and motivation to continue working towards their goals. Whether it's a personal achievement, a professional accomplishment, or progress towards a larger goal, individuals should take the time to reflect on their successes and give themselves credit for their hard work and dedication.

Building a sense of accomplishment and pride is also about recognizing one's strengths and abilities. By acknowledging their skills, talents, and qualities, individuals can develop a greater sense of self-awareness and confidence. By focusing on their strengths and leveraging them to achieve their goals, individuals can build a strong sense of pride in their abilities and accomplishments. Recognizing and embracing one's unique qualities can also help individuals build a positive self-image and increase their confidence in their ability to succeed. By setting clear and achievable goals, facing and overcoming challenges, recognizing and celebrating accomplishments, and acknowledging one's strengths and abilities, individuals can cultivate a sense of pride in their abilities and efforts. By developing a positive self-image and celebrating their successes, individuals can build confidence, motivation, and resilience that can help them achieve their goals and fulfill their potential. Building a sense of accomplishment and pride is a lifelong journey that requires dedication, perseverance, and self-reflection, but the rewards of a greater sense of self-worth and satisfaction are well worth the effort.

- Encouraging a growth mindset

Encouraging a growth mindset is a concept rooted in the belief that individuals have the ability to improve their skills and intelligence through effort and perseverance. This belief is in stark contrast to a fixed mindset, which views intelligence and abilities as innate and unchangeable. By fostering a growth mindset, individuals are more likely to embrace challenges, learn from failures, and ultimately achieve their goals. This shift in mindset has been shown to lead to increased motivation, resilience, and overall success in both academic and professional settings.

One of the key ways to encourage a growth mindset is through promoting a culture of learning and development. This can be achieved by providing opportunities for individuals to set goals, receive feedback, and engage in continuous improvement. By setting clear and attainable goals, individuals are able to track their progress and take pride in their accomplishments. Feedback, whether it be from peers, mentors, or supervisors, can help individuals identify areas for growth and provide guidance on how to improve. Additionally, creating a culture where learning is valued and celebrated can help individuals see challenges as opportunities for growth rather than obstacles to overcome.

Another important aspect of fostering a growth mindset is the language we use when providing feedback and encouragement. By praising effort, progress, and perseverance rather than innate talent, individuals are more likely to view challenges as opportunities to learn and improve. This shift in focus from praising intelligence to praising effort sends a powerful message that hard work and dedication are key drivers of success. Additionally, reframing failures as learning experiences can help individuals develop resilience and bounce back from setbacks with renewed determination.

In addition to promoting a culture of learning and using growth-oriented language, it is also important to teach individuals about the brain's ability to change and adapt. This concept, known as neuroplasticity, explains how our brains can rewire themselves in response to new experiences and challenges. By understanding that our brains are malleable and capable of growth, individuals are more likely to embrace challenges and persist in the face of obstacles. This knowledge can be empowering and serve as a powerful motivator to continue learning and improving.

Furthermore, providing opportunities for individuals to develop a growth mindset through practice and reflection can help solidify this way of thinking. Encouraging individuals to take on new challenges, learn new skills, and seek out feedback can help them build confidence in their ability to grow and improve. Additionally, engaging in regular reflection exercises, such as journaling or self-assessment, can help individuals identify their strengths and areas for growth, as well as track their progress over time. By actively engaging in these practices, individuals can develop a deeper understanding of themselves and their abilities, and ultimately cultivate a growth mindset. By promoting a culture of learning, using growth-oriented language, teaching about neuroplasticity, and providing opportunities for practice and reflection, individuals can develop the belief that they have the ability to improve and grow through effort and perseverance. This shift in mindset can lead to increased motivation, resilience, and ultimately, greater success in all areas of life. By fostering a growth mindset, we can empower individuals to embrace challenges, learn from failures, and ultimately reach their goals.

Chapter 10: Encouraging lifelong learning and growth

- FOSTERING A LOVE OF learning

Fostering a love of learning is a crucial aspect of education that can have a lasting impact on individuals throughout their lives. By instilling a passion for learning early on, educators can help students develop a curiosity and thirst for knowledge that will serve them well in academic pursuits and beyond. There are several strategies that can be employed to foster a love of learning, including creating a supportive and engaging learning environment, providing opportunities for exploration and discovery, and encouraging a growth mindset.

One of the most important ways to foster a love of learning is to create a supportive and engaging learning environment. This means creating a classroom where students feel safe, supported, and encouraged to take risks in their learning. Teachers can create this environment by building strong relationships with their students, establishing clear expectations, and providing opportunities for collaboration and peer support. By fostering a sense of community and belonging, educators can help students feel motivated and inspired to learn.

Another key strategy for fostering a love of learning is to provide opportunities for exploration and discovery. By allowing students to explore topics that interest them and pursue their own questions and interests, educators can help students develop a sense of ownership and agency in their learning. This can be done through projects, experiments, and hands-on activities that allow students to engage with the material in a meaningful and personal way. By fostering a sense of curiosity and wonder, educators can help students develop a lifelong love of learning.

Encouraging a growth mindset is another important strategy for fostering a love of learning. A growth mindset is the belief that intelligence and abilities can be developed through effort, practice, and perseverance. By encouraging students to embrace challenges, learn from their mistakes, and persist in the face of obstacles, educators can help students develop a resilient and positive attitude towards learning. This can help students build confidence in their abilities and develop a sense of mastery and achievement in their academic pursuits. By creating a supportive and engaging learning environment, providing opportunities for exploration and discovery, and encouraging a growth mindset, educators can help students develop a curiosity and thirst for knowledge that will serve them well in academic pursuits and beyond. By instilling a passion for learning early on, educators can help students develop the skills and attitudes that will enable them to thrive and succeed in their academic and personal endeavors.

- Providing opportunities for exploration and discovery

By providing opportunities for individuals to explore new ideas, environments, and experiences, we can foster creativity, curiosity, and a deeper understanding of the world around us. In this essay, we will explore the importance of providing opportunities for exploration and discovery, discuss some effective strategies for encouraging exploration, and examine the benefits that can result from embracing a mindset of curiosity and discovery.

Importance of Exploration and Discovery

Exploration and discovery are intrinsic to the human experience and are fundamental to our quest for knowledge and understanding. From a young age, we are driven by curiosity to explore the world around us, ask questions, and seek out new experiences. This natural inclination towards exploration is a powerful tool for personal growth and development, as it encourages us to step outside of our comfort zones, challenge our assumptions, and expand our horizons.

Providing opportunities for exploration and discovery is crucial for fostering creativity and innovation. When individuals are encouraged to explore new ideas and perspectives, they are more likely to think outside the box, come up with novel solutions to complex problems, and make valuable contributions to society. By creating an environment that celebrates curiosity and encourages exploration, we can cultivate a culture of innovation and creativity that benefits both individuals and organizations.

Exploration and discovery also play a key role in personal growth and development. When we step outside of our familiar surroundings and routines, we are forced to confront new challenges, adapt to unfamiliar situations, and learn from our experiences. This process of exploration can lead to increased self-awareness, resilience, and adaptability, as individuals learn to navigate the uncertainties and complexities of the world around them. By providing opportunities for exploration, we can empower individuals to push their boundaries, discover their strengths and weaknesses, and develop the skills they need to thrive in an ever-changing world.

Effective Strategies for Encouraging Exploration

There are several strategies that can be effective in encouraging exploration and discovery. One key strategy is to create an environment that is conducive to curiosity and experimentation. This can involve providing individuals with the time and resources they need to explore new ideas, engage in hands-on learning experiences, and pursue their interests and passions. By fostering a culture of curiosity, we can empower individuals to take risks, challenge the status quo, and pursue their own paths of discovery.

Another effective strategy for encouraging exploration is to provide individuals with opportunities for interdisciplinary learning and collaboration. By bringing together individuals from diverse backgrounds and disciplines, we can create a dynamic environment that stimulates creativity, fosters innovation, and encourages cross-pollination of ideas. Interdisciplinary collaboration can lead to new insights, new perspectives, and new ways of thinking that can drive breakthrough discoveries and advancements in a wide range of fields.

It is also important to provide individuals with the support and guidance they need to navigate the complexities of exploration and discovery. This can involve mentoring, coaching, and peer support, as well as access to resources and tools that can facilitate the exploration process. By supporting individuals in their quest for exploration, we can help them overcome obstacles, navigate challenges, and achieve their full potential.

Benefits of Embracing a Mindset of Curiosity and Discovery

Embracing a mindset of curiosity and discovery can have numerous benefits for individuals, organizations, and society as a whole. One of the key benefits of curiosity is that it can drive personal growth and development. When we approach the world with a sense of curiosity, we are more likely to seek out new experiences, learn from our mistakes, and push ourselves to explore our full potential. This can lead to increased self-awareness, resilience, and adaptability, as well as a greater sense of purpose and fulfillment in our lives.

Curiosity and exploration can also drive innovation and creativity. When individuals are encouraged to explore new ideas, challenge conventional wisdom, and think outside the box, they are more likely to come up with innovative solutions to complex problems. By embracing a mindset of curiosity and discovery, we can foster a culture of innovation that stimulates creativity, drives progress, and leads to breakthrough advancements in science, technology, and the arts.

In addition, curiosity and exploration can lead to a deeper understanding of the world around us. When we approach the world with an open mind and a sense of wonder, we are more likely to uncover new insights, discover hidden connections, and make meaningful discoveries. By embracing a mindset of curiosity and discovery, we can gain a richer appreciation of the complexities and beauty of the world, and develop a deeper sense of empathy and compassion for others. By encouraging individuals to explore new ideas, challenge their assumptions, and pursue their passions, we can empower them to push their boundaries, think creatively, and make meaningful contributions to society. Through effective strategies such as creating a culture of curiosity, promoting interdisciplinary collaboration, and providing support and guidance, we can help individuals embrace a mindset of curiosity and discovery that can lead to transformative experiences and breakthrough discoveries. Ultimately, by embracing a mindset of curiosity and discovery, we can unlock our full potential and create a brighter, more innovative, and more compassionate world for all.

- Encouraging boys to pursue their passions

Encouraging boys to pursue their passions is a crucial aspect of their overall development and well-being. From a young age, boys are often socialized to adhere to certain gender norms and expectations, which can limit their exploration of diverse interests and talents. By actively promoting and supporting boys in pursuing their passions, we can help them cultivate a sense of purpose, fulfillment, and confidence in their abilities.

One of the key ways to encourage boys to pursue their passions is by providing them with a safe and supportive environment in which to explore and express themselves. This can include creating opportunities for boys to engage in activities that align with their interests, whether it be sports, arts, music, or science. By fostering a sense of belonging and acceptance, boys are more likely to feel comfortable in pursuing their passions without fear of judgment or ridicule. Encouraging boys to participate in extracurricular activities that align with their interests can also help them develop important skills such as teamwork, creativity, and problem-solving.

In addition to providing a supportive environment, it is important to challenge traditional gender stereotypes and encourage boys to explore a wide range of interests and hobbies. By exposing boys to diverse role models and activities, we can help them see that there is no one "right" way to be a boy. Encouraging boys to break free from limiting gender norms can empower them to pursue their passions authentically and confidently. By challenging traditional notions of masculinity, we can create space for boys to express and explore their full range of interests and talents.

Furthermore, parents, educators, and caregivers play a crucial role in encouraging boys to pursue their passions. By actively listening to boys' interests and providing them with the resources and support they need to pursue their goals, we can help them cultivate a sense of purpose and achievement. Encouraging boys to set goals and work towards them can instill a sense of motivation and determination that will serve them well in the pursuit of their passions. Additionally, providing boys with opportunities to learn from mentors and experts in their field of interest can help them develop important skills and knowledge that will support their growth and development.

It is also important to recognize and celebrate boys' achievements and successes as they pursue their passions. By acknowledging and affirming boys' efforts and accomplishments, we can help boost their self-esteem and confidence in their abilities. Encouraging boys to take pride in their accomplishments can motivate them to continue pursuing their passions and striving for excellence. By recognizing and valuing boys' unique strengths and talents, we can help them develop a sense of identity and purpose that will guide them in their pursuit of their passions. By providing a safe and supportive environment, challenging traditional gender stereotypes, and empowering boys to set goals and work towards them, we can help boys cultivate a sense of purpose, confidence, and fulfillment. Through active encouragement and support, we can help boys explore their interests and talents, develop important skills, and ultimately, become confident and self-assured individuals who are capable of achieving their goals and pursuing their passions.

Chapter 11: Embracing differences and fostering diversity

- CELEBRATING INDIVIDUAL strengths and talents

Celebrating individual strengths and talents is a crucial aspect of fostering a positive and supportive environment in any setting, whether it be in the workplace, at school, or within a community. By recognizing and acknowledging the unique abilities and qualities that each person possesses, we can create a culture of appreciation and respect that not only boosts morale and motivation but also contributes to increased collaboration and productivity.

One of the first steps in celebrating individual strengths and talents is to shift our focus from a deficit-based mindset to one that is asset-based. Instead of dwelling on what individuals lack or where they may fall short, we should strive to identify and highlight the strengths, skills, and talents that make them stand out. This shift in perspective not only helps individuals develop a stronger sense of self-worth and confidence but also encourages them to further hone their abilities and excel in their respective areas of expertise.

In order to effectively celebrate the strengths and talents of individuals, it is important to create opportunities for recognition and validation. This can be done through regular feedback, praise, and acknowledgement of achievements, both big and small. Taking the time to actively listen to others, appreciate their contributions, and publicly commend their efforts can go a long way in boosting morale and fostering a sense of belonging and connection within a group or organization.

Furthermore, celebrating individual strengths and talents also involves providing opportunities for growth and development. By offering training, mentorship, and opportunities for advancement, we can help individuals further cultivate their skills and talents, ultimately leading to greater personal and professional success. Additionally, creating a culture of continuous learning and improvement can inspire others to strive for excellence and push themselves beyond their comfort zones.

It is also important to recognize that everyone has unique strengths and talents that may not always be immediately apparent. Some individuals may excel in creative pursuits, while others may have a knack for problem-solving or leadership. By taking the time to get to know each person on a personal level and acknowledging their individual strengths, we can create a more inclusive and supportive environment where everyone feels valued and appreciated. By recognizing and acknowledging the unique abilities that each person possesses, we can create a more inclusive and supportive environment where everyone has the opportunity to thrive and succeed. By shifting our focus from deficits to assets, providing opportunities for recognition and growth, and valuing the diverse talents of individuals, we can create a culture that celebrates the best in each and every person.

- Encouraging empathy and understanding

Empathy and understanding are crucial components of effective communication and building strong relationships. Encouraging empathy and understanding in our interactions with others can lead to a more positive and harmonious environment, both in our personal lives and in the broader community. By developing these qualities, we can foster greater connection, cooperation, and mutual respect among individuals from diverse backgrounds and perspectives.

One way to cultivate empathy and understanding is to actively listen to others. This involves giving the speaker our full attention, being present in the moment, and refraining from judgment or interruption. By truly listening to what others have to say, we can gain insights into their thoughts, feelings, and experiences, which can deepen our understanding of their perspectives and foster a sense of empathy. Active listening also demonstrates respect for the speaker and helps to create a safe space for open and honest communication.

Another key aspect of encouraging empathy and understanding is to practice empathy ourselves. This means putting ourselves in others' shoes and trying to see things from their perspective. By empathizing with others, we can better appreciate their feelings, struggles, and motivations, which can help us to respond with compassion and understanding. Empathy requires us to set aside our own biases and assumptions and to approach situations with an open mind and heart. It allows us to connect with others on a deeper level and to build stronger relationships based on mutual respect and understanding.

In addition to listening and practicing empathy, it is important to engage in meaningful dialogue with others. This involves expressing our own thoughts and feelings openly and honestly, while also being receptive to the perspectives and opinions of others. By engaging in respectful and empathetic conversations, we can learn from each other, challenge our own beliefs, and broaden our understanding of different viewpoints. Meaningful dialogue helps to bridge divides, build trust, and establish common ground, which can pave the way for greater empathy and understanding among individuals.

Empathy and understanding can also be fostered through education and awareness. By learning about different cultures, experiences, and perspectives, we can broaden our knowledge and develop a more inclusive and empathetic mindset. Education helps to challenge stereotypes, biases, and prejudices, and encourages us to approach others with openness, curiosity, and respect. By promoting diversity and inclusivity in our schools, workplaces, and communities, we can create environments that value and celebrate differences, which can lead to greater empathy and understanding among individuals. By actively listening, practicing empathy, engaging in meaningful dialogue, and promoting education and awareness, we can create a culture of empathy and understanding that values diversity, respects differences, and promotes mutual respect and compassion. By cultivating empathy and understanding in our interactions with others, we can create a more connected, compassionate, and empathetic world for all.

- Building a culture of inclusivity

Building a culture of inclusivity is a critical aspect of creating a positive and effective work environment. Inclusivity refers to the practice of valuing and respecting all individuals regardless of their background, beliefs, or identity. It involves fostering a sense of belonging and acceptance within a group or organization, where each person feels empowered to contribute their unique perspectives and experiences. By promoting inclusivity, organizations can harness the diverse talents and perspectives of their employees, leading to greater innovation, creativity, and ultimately success.

One of the key components of building a culture of inclusivity is promoting open communication and dialogue among employees. It is essential to create a safe space where individuals feel comfortable expressing their thoughts and feelings without fear of judgment or discrimination. Organizations can achieve this by fostering a culture of respect, empathy, and active listening. By encouraging employees to share their experiences and perspectives, organizations can gain a better understanding of the diverse needs and concerns of their workforce, leading to more inclusive policies and practices.

Another important aspect of building a culture of inclusivity is promoting diversity in hiring and promotion practices. Organizations should actively seek out candidates from diverse backgrounds and perspectives, ensuring that their workforce reflects the broader society. By hiring employees with a wide range of experiences and viewpoints, organizations can create a more inclusive and dynamic work environment. Additionally, organizations should provide training and development opportunities to support the career advancement of underrepresented groups, ensuring that all employees have the opportunity to succeed and grow within the organization.

In order to promote inclusivity, organizations must also address and dismantle systemic barriers and discrimination that may exist within their culture. This requires a commitment to promoting equity and fairness in all aspects of the organization, including hiring, promotion, and decision-making processes. Organizations should conduct regular assessments and audits to identify areas where bias or discrimination may be present, and take action to address and rectify these issues. By creating a more equitable and inclusive work environment, organizations can ensure that all employees have the opportunity to thrive and succeed.

In addition to addressing systemic barriers, organizations must also promote education and awareness around diversity and inclusivity. This can involve providing training and resources to employees on topics such as unconscious bias, privilege, and cultural competency. By increasing awareness and understanding of these issues, organizations can create a more inclusive and welcoming environment for all employees. Furthermore, organizations should actively celebrate and promote diversity within their workforce, recognizing the unique contributions and perspectives that each individual brings to the table.

In closing, building a culture of inclusivity requires ongoing commitment and vigilance from all levels of the organization. It is not enough to simply implement diversity and inclusion initiatives; organizations must also ensure that these efforts are integrated into all aspects of their operations and culture. This requires leadership from senior management, who must actively champion inclusivity and hold all employees accountable for promoting a culture of respect and acceptance. By creating a culture of inclusivity, organizations can foster a more diverse, innovative, and successful work environment for all employees.

Chapter 12: Supporting boys in their transition to adulthood

- HELPING BOYS NAVIGATE the challenges of adolescence

Adolescence is a critical period of development for boys, marked by physical, emotional, and cognitive changes. It is a time when boys navigate the transition from childhood to adulthood, facing a myriad of challenges along the way. As they grapple with their changing bodies, shifting social dynamics, and emerging identities, it is important for parents, educators, and other adults in their lives to provide support and guidance. By understanding the unique challenges that boys face during adolescence and adopting strategies to help them navigate these challenges, we can ensure that they emerge from this period with confidence, resilience, and a strong sense of self.

One of the key challenges that boys face during adolescence is the pressure to conform to traditional gender norms. From a young age, boys are socialized to be tough, independent, and stoic, often at the expense of their emotional well-being. As they enter adolescence, this pressure intensifies, as boys are expected to assert their masculinity through behaviors such as aggression, risk-taking, and avoidance of vulnerability. This can lead to a range of negative outcomes, including increased rates of substance abuse, delinquency, and mental health issues.

To help boys navigate the challenges of adolescence, it is important to challenge these harmful gender stereotypes and promote a more inclusive and healthy understanding of masculinity. This can involve encouraging boys to express their emotions, communicate openly about their feelings, and seek support when needed. It also involves creating environments that celebrate diversity, respect individual differences, and foster healthy relationships. By fostering a sense of belonging and acceptance, boys can feel empowered to explore their identities and navigate the complexities of adolescence in a positive and healthy way.

Another challenge that boys face during adolescence is the pressure to achieve academically and socially. As they navigate the transition to middle and high school, boys are expected to excel in their studies, participate in extracurricular activities, and build friendships and social connections. This can be overwhelming for many boys, leading to feelings of inadequacy, anxiety, and stress. Additionally, the pressures to conform to societal expectations of success can result in boys feeling isolated, disconnected, and misunderstood.

To support boys in navigating these challenges, it is important to create environments that foster a sense of belonging, inclusion, and support. This can involve providing access to academic resources, mentoring programs, and extracurricular opportunities that cater to their interests and strengths. It also involves building strong relationships with caring adults who can offer guidance, encouragement, and support. By creating a supportive network of adults and peers, boys can feel empowered to pursue their goals, build meaningful relationships, and navigate the complexities of adolescence with confidence and resilience.

In addition to academic and social pressures, boys also face unique challenges when it comes to their physical and emotional development. During adolescence, boys undergo significant changes in their bodies, including growth spurts, voice changes, and hormonal fluctuations. These changes can be disorienting and overwhelming, leading to feelings of self-consciousness, insecurity, and confusion. Additionally, boys may struggle with issues related to body image, sexuality, and identity, as they grapple with societal expectations of what it means to be a man.

To help boys navigate these challenges, it is important to provide education and support around issues of physical and emotional development. This can involve offering age-appropriate information about puberty, sexuality, and healthy relationships, as well as promoting positive body image and self-esteem. It also involves creating spaces where boys feel comfortable expressing their emotions, asking questions, and seeking guidance. By fostering open and honest conversations about these topics, boys can feel empowered to navigate their physical and emotional changes with confidence and self-awareness. As they navigate the transition from childhood to adulthood, boys face a range of pressures and expectations that can impact their well-being and self-esteem. By understanding the unique challenges that boys face during adolescence and adopting strategies to help them navigate these challenges, we can ensure that they emerge from this period with confidence, resilience, and a strong sense of self. By fostering inclusive and supportive environments, challenging harmful gender stereotypes, and promoting healthy relationships, we can empower boys to navigate the complexities of adolescence with grace and resilience.

- Building resilience for the future

In a world that is constantly changing and evolving, it is essential for individuals and organizations to build resilience in order to thrive in the face of adversity. Resilience is the ability to adapt and bounce back from difficult situations, and it is a key component of success in both personal and professional endeavors. By developing resilience, individuals can better navigate challenges, overcome setbacks, and emerge stronger and more successful than before.

One of the most important aspects of building resilience is developing a growth mindset. A growth mindset is the belief that one's abilities and intelligence can be developed through effort and perseverance. People with a growth mindset are more likely to see challenges as opportunities for growth and learning, rather than insurmountable obstacles. By cultivating a growth mindset, individuals can increase their resilience and better cope with challenges and setbacks.

Another key component of building resilience is developing strong social connections and support systems. Research has shown that people with strong social support networks are more resilient in the face of adversity. By building and maintaining strong relationships with friends, family, colleagues, and mentors, individuals can gain valuable emotional support, guidance, and encouragement during difficult times. Additionally, social connections can provide individuals with a sense of belonging and purpose, which can help them navigate challenges with greater ease.

In addition to developing a growth mindset and building strong social connections, it is important for individuals to take care of their physical and mental well-being in order to build resilience. This includes getting regular exercise, eating a healthy diet, getting enough sleep, and managing stress effectively. Research has shown that taking care of one's physical and mental health can increase resilience and help individuals better cope with challenges and setbacks. By prioritizing self-care and well-being, individuals can build the mental and emotional strength needed to navigate difficult situations with grace and resilience.

Furthermore, it is important for individuals to cultivate adaptability and flexibility in order to build resilience for the future. In today's rapidly changing world, the ability to adapt to new circumstances and embrace change is essential for success. By remaining open-minded and willing to try new things, individuals can build the resilience needed to navigate uncertainty and ambiguity with confidence and determination. Cultivating adaptability and flexibility can help individuals to thrive in the face of challenges and emerge stronger and more resilient than before. By developing a growth mindset, building strong social connections, taking care of physical and mental well-being, and cultivating adaptability and flexibility, individuals can increase their resilience and better cope with challenges and setbacks. By building resilience, individuals can navigate difficult situations with grace and determination, and emerge stronger and more successful than before. By prioritizing resilience, individuals can build the mental and emotional strength needed to thrive in the face of adversity and achieve their goals and aspirations.

- Preparing boys for independence and success

Preparing boys for independence and success is a vital aspect of parenting and education that requires careful attention and planning. In today's rapidly changing world, it is more important than ever to equip young boys with the skills and mindset necessary to navigate the challenges and opportunities that lie ahead. In order to effectively prepare boys for independence and success, it is essential to focus on nurturing key traits such as resilience, responsibility, and self-reliance. By instilling these qualities in boys from a young age, parents and educators can help them develop the confidence and competence needed to thrive in the complex and competitive world they will inherit.

One of the first steps in preparing boys for independence and success is to foster a sense of resilience. Resilience is the ability to bounce back from setbacks and adversity, and it is a crucial skill for navigating the ups and downs of life.

By teaching boys how to effectively cope with challenges and setbacks, parents and educators can help them develop the mental toughness and determination needed to persevere in the face of obstacles. Encouraging boys to take risks and try new things, while providing support and guidance when they encounter difficulties, can help them build their resilience muscle and learn to see setbacks as opportunities for growth and learning.

Another important aspect of preparing boys for independence and success is to instill a sense of responsibility. Responsibility involves taking ownership of one's actions and decisions, and it is a key trait for leading a successful and fulfilling life. By teaching boys the importance of accountability and self-discipline, parents and educators can help them develop a strong sense of personal responsibility that will serve them well in their future endeavors. Encouraging boys to set goals, make plans, and follow through on their commitments can help them develop the skills and habits necessary to take charge of their lives and achieve their ambitions.

In addition to resilience and responsibility, cultivating self-reliance is also essential for preparing boys for independence and success. Self-reliance involves having the confidence and ability to rely on oneself to achieve goals and solve problems, and it is a critical trait for navigating the complexities of adult life. By encouraging boys to become independent thinkers and problem solvers, parents and educators can help them develop the skills and mindset needed to thrive in an increasingly complex and interconnected world. Providing boys with opportunities to make decisions, take initiative, and learn from their mistakes can help them develop the self-reliance and resourcefulness necessary to succeed in any endeavor they choose to pursue. By focusing on nurturing key traits such as resilience, responsibility, and self-reliance, parents and educators can help boys develop the skills and mindset needed to thrive in the rapidly changing world they will inherit. By instilling these qualities in boys from a young age and providing them with the support and guidance they need to navigate the challenges and opportunities that lie ahead, we can help them reach their full potential and lead successful and fulfilling lives. Through a combination of encouragement, support, and empowerment, we can help boys grow into confident, capable, and resilient individuals who are equipped to take on the world and create a brighter future for themselves and others.

Chapter 13: Cultivating a sense of purpose and meaning

- HELPING BOYS FIND their passion and purpose

Boys, like all individuals, have unique interests, talents, and aspirations that shape their sense of purpose and passion in life. However, finding one's passion and purpose can be a challenging journey, especially for young boys who may face societal pressures and expectations that can influence their choices and decisions. As educators, parents, and mentors, it is important for us to support and guide boys in discovering and pursuing their passions, helping them to cultivate a sense of purpose and fulfillment in their lives.

One of the key ways to help boys find their passion and purpose is to encourage them to explore a wide range of activities and interests. By exposing boys to different opportunities and experiences, we can help them discover what truly excites and motivates them. Whether it is through sports, arts, music, science, or any other field, boys should be encouraged to try new things and find activities that resonate with their interests and talents. By fostering a spirit of curiosity and exploration, we can help boys uncover their passion and purpose in life.

In addition to exploration, it is important to provide boys with the support and encouragement they need to pursue their interests and goals. For many boys, finding their passion and purpose may require overcoming obstacles and challenges, such as self-doubt, fear of failure, or external pressures. As mentors and role models, we can help boys build the resilience and determination they need to pursue their passions, even in the face of adversity. By offering guidance, feedback, and encouragement, we can empower boys to pursue their dreams and ambitions with confidence and conviction.

Furthermore, it is essential to create a supportive and nurturing environment for boys to explore and express their passions. Boys may face social norms and expectations that discourage them from pursuing certain interests or activities, especially those that are traditionally associated with girls or seen as "unmanly. " As parents, educators, and mentors, we must challenge these stereotypes and create a safe space for boys to explore and develop their passions. By fostering an inclusive and accepting environment, we can help boys feel comfortable and empowered to follow their dreams, no matter what they may be.

Moreover, it is crucial to help boys cultivate a sense of purpose and meaning in their lives by connecting their passions to a larger cause or goal. By encouraging boys to think about how their interests and talents can contribute to the greater good, we can help them develop a sense of purpose that goes beyond personal fulfillment. Whether it is through community service, advocacy, or leadership roles, boys can find meaning and fulfillment by using their passions to make a positive impact on the world. By helping boys see the connection between their passions and a higher purpose, we can empower them to lead purposeful and meaningful lives. By encouraging boys to explore their interests, providing them with the support they need to pursue their goals, creating a nurturing environment for them to express their passions, and helping them connect their interests to a larger purpose, we can empower boys to discover and follow their dreams. Ultimately, by helping boys find their passion and purpose, we can enable them to lead fulfilling, meaningful, and purposeful lives.

- Encouraging boys to make a positive difference in the world

Encouraging boys to make a positive difference in the world is a crucial aspect of fostering a society that values equality, empathy, and social responsibility. Historically, boys have been socialized to prioritize traits such as aggression, competition, and dominance, which can contribute to negative behaviors and attitudes. However, by shifting societal norms and expectations, we can empower boys to embrace qualities such as kindness, compassion, and cooperation that are essential for creating a more harmonious and equitable world.

One key strategy for encouraging boys to make a positive difference in the world is to provide them with positive male role models who exemplify traits such as empathy, integrity, and respect for others. By showcasing examples of men who have made significant contributions to society through acts of kindness and compassion, boys can see that these qualities are not only admirable but also achievable. Additionally, involving boys in mentorship programs or leadership initiatives where they can learn from and be inspired by positive male role models can help them develop the skills and values necessary to make a positive impact in their communities.

Another important aspect of encouraging boys to make a positive difference in the world is to educate them about the importance of gender equality and social justice. By teaching boys about the systemic inequalities and injustices that exist in society, we can help them understand the importance of standing up for the rights and dignity of all people, regardless of gender, race, or socioeconomic status. Furthermore, providing boys with opportunities to engage in discussions and activities that promote empathy, understanding, and mutual respect can help them develop the critical thinking skills and self-awareness needed to address issues of inequality and discrimination in their own lives and communities.

In addition to providing boys with positive role models and education on social issues, it is also essential to create inclusive and supportive environments that empower boys to express their emotions, explore their interests, and develop their talents. By challenging traditional gender stereotypes and expectations that limit boys' self-expression and potential, we can create spaces where boys feel comfortable being vulnerable, creative, and authentic. Encouraging boys to participate in activities that promote collaboration, communication, and emotional intelligence, such as sports, arts, and community service, can help them develop the confidence, skills, and values needed to make a positive difference in the world. By providing boys with positive male role models, educating them about the importance of gender equality and social justice, and creating spaces where they can express themselves authentically and develop their talents, we can empower boys to become compassionate, empathetic, and responsible members of society who contribute to a more just and equitable world.

- Building a sense of fulfillment and contentment

Building a sense of fulfillment and contentment is a lifelong journey that requires self-awareness, reflection, and intentional actions. It is not a destination to be reached, but rather a continuous process of growth and discovery. Fulfillment is defined as a feeling of satisfaction and happiness derived from achieving one's goals and expectations, while contentment is characterized by a sense of peace and acceptance of one's current circumstances. Together, these two components create a profound sense of inner well-being and harmony that can enrich every aspect of our lives.

The first step in building a sense of fulfillment and contentment is to cultivate self-awareness. This involves taking the time to reflect on our values, beliefs, strengths, and weaknesses. By understanding what truly matters to us and what brings us joy and fulfillment, we can make more informed decisions that align with our authentic selves. Self-awareness also allows us to recognize patterns of behavior that may be holding us back from experiencing true contentment. By identifying and addressing these patterns, we can begin to make positive changes that will lead to a more fulfilling life.

Another important aspect of building a sense of fulfillment and contentment is setting meaningful goals and working towards achieving them. Goals give us a sense of purpose and direction, and they provide motivation to overcome obstacles and challenges. It is essential to set goals that are realistic, measurable, and aligned with our values and aspirations. By breaking larger goals down into smaller, manageable tasks, we can create a clear path towards success and experience a sense of accomplishment along the way. Celebrating our achievements, no matter how small, can help to reinforce our sense of fulfillment and keep us motivated to continue moving forward.

In addition to setting goals, it is important to cultivate a sense of gratitude and appreciation for the present moment. Practicing mindfulness and being fully present in the here and now can help us to appreciate the beauty and joy that surrounds us every day. By focusing on the positive aspects of our lives and expressing gratitude for the blessings we have received, we can cultivate a sense of contentment and fulfillment that transcends external circumstances. Simply taking the time to pause and reflect on the things we are grateful for can shift our perspective and bring a sense of peace and fulfillment.

Building strong relationships and connections with others is another key component of building a sense of fulfillment and contentment. Humans are social beings, and meaningful connections with others can bring a sense of joy, belonging, and purpose to our lives. By nurturing our relationships with friends, family, and colleagues, we can create a support system that helps us to navigate life's challenges and celebrate our successes. Investing time and energy in building and maintaining these connections can lead to deeper levels of fulfillment and contentment that enrich our lives in profound ways.

To recapitulate, it is important to prioritize self-care and well-being in the pursuit of fulfillment and contentment. Taking care of our physical, emotional, and mental health is essential for maintaining a balanced and fulfilling life. This may involve engaging in regular exercise, eating nutritious foods, getting enough sleep, and practicing stress-relief techniques such as meditation or yoga. It is also important to make time for activities that bring us joy and relaxation, whether it be reading a book, listening to music, or spending time in nature. By prioritizing our own well-being, we can cultivate a sense of inner peace and contentment that radiates outwards and positively impacts every aspect of our lives. By cultivating self-awareness, setting meaningful goals, practicing gratitude, nurturing relationships, and prioritizing self-care, we can create a life that is rich in purpose, joy, and fulfillment. It is never too late to start this journey towards a more fulfilling and contented life, and by taking small steps each day, we can gradually build a sense of inner well-being that sustains us through life's ups and downs. Remember, fulfillment and contentment are not destinations to be reached, but rather a continuous process of growth and discovery that enriches our lives in profound ways.

Chapter 14: Nurturing boys' creativity and innovation

- FOSTERING CREATIVE expression and exploration

Fostering creative expression and exploration is essential in today's fast-paced and rapidly changing world. Creativity is a valuable skill that allows individuals to think outside the box, come up with innovative solutions, and express themselves in meaningful ways. By encouraging creativity, we can cultivate a society of forward-thinkers, problem solvers, and innovators who are capable of adapting to new challenges and opportunities.

One of the key ways to foster creative expression and exploration is through education. Schools and educational institutions play a crucial role in nurturing creativity in students by providing opportunities for them to explore different ideas, experiment with new concepts, and develop their creative skills. Teachers can encourage creativity in the classroom by creating a supportive and open-minded learning environment, where students feel free to express themselves and take risks in their learning.

In addition to formal education, organizations and businesses can also play a role in fostering creative expression and exploration among their employees. By promoting a culture of creativity and innovation, companies can inspire their employees to think creatively, come up with new ideas, and push the boundaries of traditional thinking. Employers can encourage creativity in the workplace by providing opportunities for employees to collaborate, brainstorm, and experiment with new ways of approaching problems.

Furthermore, fostering creative expression and exploration also requires individuals to cultivate a mindset of curiosity, experimentation, and openness to new ideas. By encouraging individuals to explore their interests, try new things, and step out of their comfort zones, we can help them unleash their creative potential and discover new possibilities. Creativity is not just about coming up with new ideas; it is also about being willing to take risks, fail, and learn from mistakes in order to grow and expand one's creative abilities. By encouraging creativity, we can empower individuals to think outside the box, come up with innovative solutions, and express themselves in meaningful ways. This can lead to a more innovative, adaptable, and resilient society that is better equipped to navigate the challenges and opportunities of the modern world. It is important for all of us to embrace our creative potential and cultivate a culture of creativity and exploration in order to thrive and succeed in an ever-changing world.

- Encouraging innovative thinking and problem-solving

In today's fast-paced and constantly evolving world, innovative thinking and problem-solving have become crucial skills for individuals and organizations to thrive. Encouraging a culture of innovation within a company can lead to breakthrough solutions, increased productivity, and a competitive edge in the marketplace. However, fostering an environment that nurtures creativity and out-of-the-box thinking is easier said than done. It requires a concerted effort from leadership, a supportive company culture, and individual employees who are willing to step outside their comfort zones.

One of the key elements in encouraging innovative thinking and problem-solving is leadership buy-in. Leaders play a critical role in setting the tone for the organization and creating an environment where creativity is valued and rewarded. They must communicate the importance of innovation to their teams and provide the resources and support necessary to foster a culture of creativity. This can involve setting aside time for brainstorming sessions, providing training in creative thinking techniques, and recognizing and celebrating innovative ideas and solutions. By demonstrating a commitment to innovation from the top down, leaders can inspire their teams to think differently and approach problems with a fresh perspective.

Another important factor in encouraging innovation is establishing a supportive company culture. Employees need to feel that they have the freedom to experiment, take risks, and fail without fear of repercussions. This can be achieved by promoting a growth mindset, where mistakes are seen as learning opportunities and feedback is constructive rather than critical. Encouraging collaboration and cross-functional teamwork can also help spark new ideas and perspectives, as diverse teams are more likely to come up with innovative solutions. Creating a physical workspace that fosters creativity, such as open office layouts or designated brainstorming areas, can also help stimulate innovative thinking and problem-solving.

Individual employees also play a key role in fostering innovation within an organization. It requires a willingness to challenge the status quo, think outside the box, and take risks. This can be intimidating for some employees, especially those who are more comfortable with established ways of working. Encouraging employees to step outside their comfort zones and try new approaches can help them develop their creative thinking skills and problem-solving abilities. Providing opportunities for continuous learning and development can also help employees build the confidence and knowledge they need to innovate effectively. By creating an environment that values and rewards creativity, organizations can tap into the full potential of their employees and drive innovation forward. Investing in training, resources, and support for creative thinking can pay dividends in the form of breakthrough solutions, increased productivity, and a competitive edge in the marketplace. It is a journey that requires ongoing commitment and effort, but the rewards of fostering a culture of innovation are well worth it.

- Cultivating a culture of creativity and innovation

In today's rapidly changing and competitive business landscape, cultivating a culture of creativity and innovation has become essential for organizations looking to stay ahead of the curve. Creativity and innovation are not just buzzwords; they are crucial components of success in the modern world. By fostering a culture that values and encourages creative thinking and innovation, companies can unlock new opportunities, solve complex problems, and drive growth and competitiveness.

One of the key aspects of cultivating a culture of creativity and innovation is creating an environment that empowers employees to think outside the box and take risks. This means breaking free from traditional hierarchical structures and fostering a culture of collaboration, openness, and experimentation. When employees feel supported and encouraged to explore new ideas, they are more likely to come up with innovative solutions to challenges and drive meaningful change within the organization.

Another important factor in fostering a culture of creativity and innovation is promoting diversity and inclusion within the workplace. Research has shown that diverse teams are more likely to generate innovative ideas and outperform homogeneous teams. By embracing diversity in all its forms – including diverse backgrounds, perspectives, and ways of thinking – organizations can tap into a wealth of ideas and creativity that can propel them forward. Inclusivity is also key, as all employees should feel valued, respected, and empowered to contribute to the creative process.

Furthermore, leaders play a crucial role in shaping the culture of creativity and innovation within an organization. It is essential for leaders to lead by example and demonstrate a commitment to creativity and innovation in their own work. By setting a clear vision and fostering a supportive and inclusive environment, leaders can inspire and motivate employees to think creatively and take risks. Additionally, leaders should provide the necessary resources and support to enable employees to innovate and experiment without fear of failure.

Creating a culture of creativity and innovation also requires a focus on continuous learning and development. Organizations should invest in training programs and opportunities for employees to expand their skills, learn new technologies, and stay abreast of industry trends. By encouraging lifelong learning and a growth mindset, organizations can cultivate a workforce that is adaptable, resilient, and capable of driving innovation in a constantly evolving business landscape. By creating an environment that empowers employees to think creatively, take risks, and collaborate effectively, companies can unlock new opportunities, drive growth, and stay ahead of the competition. With the right leadership, a focus on diversity and inclusion, and a commitment to continuous learning and development, organizations can foster a culture of creativity and innovation that propels them to success.

Chapter 15: Supporting boys in their academic and career pursuits

- HELPING BOYS SET AND achieve academic goals

Setting and achieving academic goals is an essential component of a successful educational journey for students of all genders. However, research has shown that boys may face unique challenges in this regard, and may require specific support and guidance to effectively set and achieve their academic goals. In this paper, we will explore some of the reasons why boys may struggle with goal-setting and achievement, as well as evaluate strategies and interventions that can help boys overcome these challenges and reach their full academic potential.

One factor that may contribute to boys' difficulties in setting and achieving academic goals is societal expectations and stereotypes surrounding masculinity. Boys are often socialized to be tough, independent, and self-reliant, which can lead to a reluctance to ask for help or seek support when facing academic challenges. This can result in boys feeling overwhelmed and isolated, and may lead to a lack of motivation and engagement in their academic pursuits. In order to address this issue, it is important for educators and parents to encourage boys to prioritize their academic goals and to create a supportive environment where they feel comfortable seeking help and guidance when needed.

Additionally, boys may struggle with goal-setting and achievement due to differences in learning styles and preferences. Research has shown that boys tend to be more kinesthetic and spatial learners, meaning they learn best through hands-on activities and visual aids. Traditional academic settings, which often prioritize verbal and auditory learning styles, may not cater to the needs of these students, leading to disengagement and underachievement. To help boys set and achieve their academic goals, educators can incorporate more hands-on activities and visual aids into their teaching practices, allowing boys to engage with the material in a way that aligns with their preferred learning style.

Furthermore, boys may face external factors that can impede their ability to set and achieve academic goals, such as peer pressure, distractions, and competing priorities. The pressure to conform to societal expectations of masculinity, coupled with the distractions of technology and social media, can make it challenging for boys to stay focused and motivated on their academic goals. Additionally, boys may have competing priorities, such as sports or extracurricular activities, that can take away time and energy from their academic pursuits. In order to help boys navigate these challenges and set realistic academic goals, it is important for educators and parents to encourage time management and prioritization skills, as well as provide support and guidance in balancing academic and extracurricular commitments.

In addition to addressing the unique challenges that boys may face in setting and achieving academic goals, it is important to provide them with the necessary tools and strategies to succeed. One effective approach is to help boys develop a growth mindset, which emphasizes the belief that abilities can be developed through dedication and hard work. By fostering a growth mindset in boys, educators and parents can help them overcome setbacks and challenges, and stay motivated and resilient in pursuit of their academic goals. Encouraging boys to set specific, measurable, achievable, relevant, and time-bound (SMART) goals can also help them stay focused and accountable in their academic pursuits. By breaking down larger goals into smaller, more manageable tasks, boys can track their progress and celebrate their achievements along the way. By creating a supportive and engaging learning environment, tailoring teaching practices to boys' preferred learning styles, and fostering a growth mindset and goal-setting skills, educators and parents can empower boys to reach their full academic potential. By investing in the academic success of boys, we can help them overcome barriers and achieve their goals, ultimately setting them on a path to a bright and successful future.

- Building skills for success in the workplace

In today's competitive job market, having the right skills is essential for success in the workplace. Employers are looking for candidates who possess a diverse set of skills that go beyond just technical knowledge. Building skills for success in the workplace requires a combination of hard and soft skills that can help individuals thrive in their careers and stand out from the crowd.

One of the key skills that is essential for success in the workplace is effective communication. Good communication skills are crucial in any job, as they enable individuals to effectively convey their ideas, thoughts, and information to colleagues, clients, and supervisors. Being able to communicate clearly and concisely can help to avoid misunderstandings and ensure that everyone is on the same page. In addition, effective communication skills can also help individuals to build strong relationships with their coworkers and create a positive work environment.

Another important skill for success in the workplace is problem-solving. In any job, there will inevitably be challenges and obstacles that arise, and being able to effectively problem solve is crucial for overcoming these challenges. Problem-solving skills involve being able to analyze a situation, identify the root cause of the problem, and come up with creative solutions to address it. Individuals who possess strong problem-solving skills are able to adapt to changes in the workplace quickly and efficiently, which can set them apart from their peers.

Time management is also a critical skill for success in the workplace. In a fast-paced work environment, individuals are often juggling multiple tasks and deadlines, and being able to effectively manage their time is essential for staying organized and productive. Time management skills involve setting priorities, creating a schedule, and being able to prioritize tasks based on their importance and urgency. By effectively managing their time, individuals can maximize their productivity and ensure that they are able to meet deadlines and deliver high-quality work.

Adaptability is another key skill for success in the workplace. In today's ever-changing work environment, the ability to adapt to new situations and challenges is essential for staying relevant and competitive. Individuals who are adaptable are able to embrace change, learn new skills, and evolve with the needs of their organization. Being adaptable also involves being open to feedback and constructive criticism, and being able to adjust their approach based on new information. Employers value individuals who are adaptable, as they are able to thrive in dynamic work environments and contribute to the success of their team.

Collaboration is another important skill for success in the workplace. In today's interconnected world, teamwork is essential for achieving goals and driving innovation. Individuals who are able to collaborate effectively with their colleagues bring diverse perspectives and ideas to the table, which can lead to more creative solutions and better outcomes. Collaboration involves being able to communicate effectively, listen to others, and work together towards a common goal. By fostering a collaborative work environment, individuals can build strong relationships with their colleagues and contribute to the overall success of their team. Effective communication, problem-solving, time management, adaptability, and collaboration are all key skills that can help individuals achieve success in their careers. By developing these skills and continually seeking ways to improve and grow, individuals can position themselves for success in today's competitive job market.

- Encouraging lifelong learning and growth

Lifelong learning and personal growth are essential components of a fulfilling and successful life. Encouraging individuals to continuously seek out new knowledge and experiences can lead to personal and professional development, as well as increased satisfaction and fulfillment. In today's rapidly changing world, where technology and societal norms are constantly evolving, the ability to adapt and learn new skills is more important than ever. By fostering a culture of lifelong learning and growth, individuals can stay relevant in their careers, maintain a curious and open mindset, and continue to expand their horizons.

There are many benefits to encouraging lifelong learning and growth in individuals. One of the most significant advantages is the opportunity for personal development and self-improvement. When individuals commit to ongoing education and skill development, they are able to expand their knowledge and capabilities, enabling them to take on new challenges and pursue their goals with confidence. Lifelong learning can also help individuals stay mentally sharp and engaged, leading to improved cognitive function and overall well-being. In addition, continuous learning can enhance personal and professional relationships, as individuals are able to communicate more effectively and understand different perspectives.

Furthermore, embracing a mindset of lifelong learning can help individuals adapt to change and navigate uncertainty with greater ease. With the rapid pace of technological advancements and changing job markets, the ability to learn new skills and adapt to new environments is crucial for long-term success. By maintaining a commitment to ongoing education and growth, individuals can future-proof their careers and remain competitive in their respective fields. Continuous learning also allows individuals to stay informed about current trends and developments, enabling them to make informed decisions and seize new opportunities as they arise.

In addition to the personal benefits of lifelong learning, there are also societal advantages to fostering a culture of growth and education. Lifelong learners are more likely to be engaged citizens who contribute positively to their communities and society as a whole. By staying informed and educated, individuals can participate in meaningful discussions, advocate for social change, and make informed decisions that benefit their communities. Furthermore, lifelong learning can help bridge social divides and promote greater understanding and empathy among diverse populations. By encouraging individuals to seek out new knowledge and perspectives, we can create a more inclusive and cohesive society.

There are several practical strategies that can be employed to encourage lifelong learning and growth in individuals. One effective approach is to provide access to educational resources and opportunities for skill development. This can include offering workshops, seminars, and online courses that cover a wide range of topics, as well as promoting continued education through formal degree programs or certification courses. Employers can also support lifelong learning by investing in employee training and development programs, which can help employees stay relevant in their roles and advance their careers.

Another important aspect of fostering lifelong learning is to create a supportive and inclusive learning environment. This can involve promoting a culture of curiosity and learning within organizations, schools, and communities, where individuals feel empowered to ask questions, explore new ideas, and take risks. By creating a safe and welcoming space for learning, individuals are more likely to feel motivated and inspired to pursue their educational goals. Additionally, providing mentorship and guidance from experienced educators and professionals can help individuals navigate their learning journey and overcome any obstacles they may encounter. By fostering a culture of continuous education and skill development, individuals can enhance their knowledge and capabilities, adapt to change with greater ease, and contribute positively to their communities. Through providing access to educational resources, creating a supportive learning environment, and promoting a mindset of curiosity and exploration, we can empower individuals to thrive in today's ever-changing world. Ultimately, lifelong learning is not just a means to an end, but a journey of self-discovery and personal growth that can lead to a more fulfilling and purposeful life.

Chapter 16: Building resilience through adversity

- TEACHING BOYS TO BOUNCE back from setbacks

Teaching boys to bounce back from setbacks is a crucial aspect of their development and growth. In today's fast-paced and competitive world, the ability to recover from failures and setbacks is a valuable skill that can determine a person's success in various aspects of life. Boys, in particular, can benefit greatly from learning how to effectively deal with setbacks and adversity, as it can help them build resilience, confidence, and perseverance.

One of the key factors in teaching boys to bounce back from setbacks is promoting a growth mindset. This mindset emphasizes the idea that intelligence, abilities, and skills are not fixed traits but can be developed through effort, perseverance, and learning from failures. By instilling a growth mindset in boys, we can help them view setbacks as opportunities for growth and learning rather than insurmountable obstacles. This can help boys develop a positive attitude towards challenges and setbacks, fostering resilience and perseverance in the face of adversity.

Another important aspect of teaching boys to bounce back from setbacks is teaching them how to effectively manage their emotions. Setbacks and failures can often trigger strong emotions such as frustration, anger, disappointment, and self-doubt. It is important for boys to learn how to recognize and manage these emotions in a healthy way, rather than letting them overwhelm and paralyze them. By helping boys develop emotional intelligence and coping skills, we can empower them to navigate setbacks with resilience and grace.

In addition, teaching boys to bounce back from setbacks involves helping them develop problem-solving skills and a solution-focused mindset. When faced with a setback, boys should be encouraged to approach the situation with a proactive attitude, focusing on finding solutions and taking positive steps towards overcoming the obstacle. By teaching boys how to break down problems, identify possible solutions, and take action to address them, we can help them build confidence in their ability to overcome challenges and setbacks.

Furthermore, it is important to foster a supportive and nurturing environment for boys as they learn to bounce back from setbacks. Boys need to know that they have a safe space where they can express their emotions, seek guidance and support, and receive encouragement and validation. By providing boys with a supportive network of adults, mentors, peers, and resources, we can help them build resilience and confidence in their ability to bounce back from setbacks.

Ultimately, teaching boys to bounce back from setbacks is an ongoing process that requires patience, consistency, and active involvement from parents, educators, mentors, and other caring adults. By fostering a growth mindset, promoting emotional intelligence, teaching problem-solving skills, and providing a supportive environment, we can empower boys to build resilience, confidence, and perseverance in the face of adversity. Through these efforts, we can help boys develop the skills they need to navigate life's challenges with resilience and grace.

- Helping boys develop a growth mindset

Boys, like all children, possess incredible potential for growth and development. However, it is crucial that we as educators, parents, and mentors provide them with the tools and support needed to cultivate a growth mindset. A growth mindset is the belief that abilities and intelligence can be developed through hard work, perseverance, and dedication. This mindset not only improves academic performance but also fosters resilience, grit, and a love for learning. In this article, we will explore several strategies to help boys develop a growth mindset and reach their full potential.

One of the most effective ways to help boys develop a growth mindset is to praise their efforts and strategies rather than their intelligence or talent. Research has shown that praising effort and perseverance can enhance motivation and promote a positive attitude towards learning. When boys are praised for their hard work and determination, they are more likely to embrace challenges, see failures as opportunities for growth, and persist in the face of setbacks. On the other hand, when boys are praised for their intelligence or talent, they may develop a fixed mindset and become afraid of making mistakes or taking risks. Therefore, it is important to be mindful of the language we use when providing feedback to boys and to focus on the process rather than the outcome.

Another key strategy for helping boys develop a growth mindset is to teach them about the brain and how it changes and grows with practice. By explaining the concept of neuroplasticity – the brain's ability to reorganize itself in response to new experiences – boys can better understand that their abilities are not fixed but can be improved with effort and dedication. This knowledge can empower boys to take ownership of their learning and development and instill a sense of agency and control over their academic performance. Additionally, teaching boys about the importance of adopting a growth mindset can help them develop the resilience and perseverance needed to navigate the challenges and obstacles they may encounter in their educational journey.

Furthermore, creating a supportive and nurturing learning environment is essential for fostering a growth mindset in boys. Boys thrive in environments where they feel safe, respected, and valued, and where they are encouraged to take risks, make mistakes, and learn from their failures. By creating a culture of curiosity, exploration, and growth, educators and parents can help boys develop a love for learning and a willingness to try new things. Providing opportunities for collaborative learning, hands-on experiences, and creative expression can also fuel boys' passion for learning and foster a growth mindset. Additionally, offering boys positive role models and mentors who embody a growth mindset can inspire and motivate them to reach their full potential.

In addition to these strategies, it is important to involve boys in setting goals and tracking their progress towards achieving them. By encouraging boys to set specific, achievable, and challenging goals, they can develop a sense of purpose, direction, and motivation. Regularly reviewing and reflecting on their progress can help boys stay focused, motivated, and accountable for their learning. Moreover, celebrating their achievements, big or small, can boost boys' confidence and self-esteem and reinforce their belief in their ability to succeed. By involving boys in the goal-setting process and empowering them to take ownership of their learning, we can help them develop the resilience, grit, and determination needed to overcome obstacles and achieve their aspirations. By praising their efforts and strategies, teaching them about the brain's capacity for growth, creating a supportive learning environment, involving them in goal-setting, and celebrating their achievements, we can empower boys to embrace challenges, learn from failures, and strive for excellence. With the right tools, support, and guidance, boys can cultivate a growth mindset and unlock their full potential. Let us empower our boys to believe in themselves, pursue their dreams, and become lifelong learners.

- Encouraging perseverance and determination

Encouraging perseverance and determination is essential for achieving success in both personal and professional endeavors. Perseverance refers to the ability to keep going in the face of obstacles and setbacks, while determination is the commitment to achieving a goal despite challenges. These qualities are crucial in overcoming adversity and achieving long-term goals.

One way to encourage perseverance and determination is to set clear and achievable goals. When individuals have a clear vision of what they want to achieve, they are more motivated to persist through challenges and setbacks. It is important to break down larger goals into smaller, manageable tasks that can be completed step by step. By achieving small victories along the way, individuals are able to build momentum and stay motivated.

Another key factor in encouraging perseverance and determination is to cultivate a growth mindset. This mindset is based on the belief that intelligence and abilities can be developed through effort and hard work. When individuals have a growth mindset, they are more likely to view setbacks as opportunities for growth and learning, rather than insurmountable obstacles. Encouraging individuals to embrace challenges and see failures as opportunities for growth can help foster a sense of perseverance and determination.

In addition to setting clear goals and cultivating a growth mindset, social support is also crucial in encouraging perseverance and determination. Surrounding oneself with a supportive network of friends, family, and mentors can provide encouragement, guidance, and motivation during difficult times.

Having someone to lean on during challenging moments can help individuals stay motivated and focused on their goals.

Furthermore, it is important to celebrate progress and achievements along the way. Recognizing and acknowledging small victories can help boost motivation and confidence, reinforcing the belief that perseverance and determination are paying off. By celebrating even the smallest accomplishments, individuals can stay motivated and focused on their long-term goals.

Lastly, self-care is essential in encouraging perseverance and determination. Taking care of one's physical and mental well-being is crucial for maintaining high levels of motivation and resilience in the face of challenges. Regular exercise, healthy eating, and adequate rest can help individuals stay energized and focused on their goals. Additionally, practicing mindfulness and stress-reducing activities such as meditation or yoga can help individuals stay centered and grounded during difficult times. By setting clear goals, cultivating a growth mindset, seeking social support, celebrating progress, and practicing self-care, individuals can foster a sense of resilience and motivation that will help them overcome challenges and achieve their long-term goals. With the right mindset and support system in place, individuals can tackle obstacles with confidence and determination, ultimately leading to greater success and fulfillment in life.

Chapter 17: Promoting physical health and well-being

- EMPHASIZING THE IMPORTANCE of physical activity and nutrition

Physical activity and nutrition are essential components of a healthy lifestyle. It is widely recognized that both regular exercise and a balanced diet are crucial for maintaining overall health and well-being. In today's fast-paced world, it can be easy to overlook the importance of these factors, but incorporating them into our daily routines is vital for longevity and quality of life.

Regular physical activity has numerous benefits for both the body and mind. It helps to improve cardiovascular health, strengthen muscles and bones, and boost immune function. Exercise also plays a key role in managing weight and reducing the risk of chronic diseases such as diabetes, heart disease, and certain types of cancer. Additionally, physical activity has been shown to have a positive impact on mental health, reducing symptoms of anxiety and depression and improving cognitive function.

Incorporating exercise into your daily routine doesn't have to be complicated or time-consuming. Even simple activities like walking, cycling, or gardening can have a significant impact on your overall health. Aim for at least 150 minutes of moderate-intensity exercise per week, such as brisk walking or swimming, and incorporate strength training exercises at least twice a week to build muscle mass and improve bone density. Remember to consult with a healthcare provider before starting any new exercise regimen, especially if you have underlying health conditions or are currently inactive.

In addition to regular physical activity, maintaining a healthy diet is crucial for overall health and well-being. A balanced diet should include a variety of foods from all the major food groups, such as fruits, vegetables, whole grains, lean proteins, and healthy fats. It is important to limit the intake of processed foods, sugary drinks, and foods high in saturated fats and added sugars, as these can contribute to weight gain and increase the risk of chronic diseases.

Eating a well-rounded diet provides essential nutrients that are necessary for maintaining optimal health. Vitamins, minerals, and antioxidants found in fruits and vegetables help to boost the immune system, protect against inflammation, and promote healthy skin and hair. Fiber-rich foods like whole grains, legumes, and nuts support digestive health and can help to regulate blood sugar levels. Protein sources like lean meats, poultry, fish, and plant-based proteins are essential for muscle growth and repair.

When planning meals, aim for a variety of colors on your plate to ensure a diverse range of nutrients. Incorporate foods high in vitamins A, C, and E, as well as minerals like calcium, magnesium, and zinc for optimal health. Remember to hydrate properly by drinking plenty of water throughout the day, as dehydration can have negative effects on physical performance and overall well-being. By incorporating regular exercise and a balanced diet into your daily routine, you can improve your overall health and well-being, reduce the risk of chronic diseases, and enhance your quality of life. Remember to consult with a healthcare provider or registered dietitian before making any significant changes to your exercise or dietary habits. Start slowly, set realistic goals, and stay consistent in your efforts to prioritize your health and wellness. By prioritizing physical activity and nutrition, you can take control of your health and set yourself on the path to a healthier and happier life.

- **Teaching healthy habits and self-care practices**

Teaching healthy habits and self-care practices is crucial in today's fast-paced and stressful world. It is important for individuals to prioritize their physical, mental, and emotional well-being in order to lead a fulfilling and balanced life. By instilling healthy habits and self-care practices early on, individuals can develop the tools and strategies needed to navigate life's challenges with resilience and grace.

One of the key components of teaching healthy habits and self-care practices is promoting a balanced lifestyle. This includes prioritizing proper nutrition, regular exercise, and adequate rest. Eating a balanced diet rich in fruits, vegetables, whole grains, and lean proteins can provide the necessary nutrients for optimal health and well-being. Regular exercise, whether it be a daily walk, yoga practice, or gym workout, can help improve physical fitness, reduce stress, and boost mood. Getting an adequate amount of rest each night is also crucial for overall health and well-being, as it allows the body to repair and recharge for the next day.

In addition to promoting a balanced lifestyle, teaching healthy habits and self-care practices also involves the importance of mental and emotional well-being. Practicing mindfulness, meditation, and relaxation techniques can help individuals manage stress, improve mental clarity, and enhance overall well-being. Taking time for self-reflection and self-care activities, such as reading a book, taking a hot bath, or going for a nature walk, can also help individuals recharge and rejuvenate their minds and bodies. By prioritizing mental and emotional well-being, individuals can build resilience and coping strategies to better navigate life's ups and downs.

Another important aspect of teaching healthy habits and self-care practices is promoting positive relationships and social connections. Building strong social connections and maintaining supportive relationships can help individuals feel connected, valued, and supported. Spending time with friends and loved ones, participating in social activities, and joining community groups can help individuals feel a sense of belonging and connection. Additionally, fostering positive relationships can provide emotional support, encouragement, and a sense of community, which are essential for overall well-being.

In order to effectively teach healthy habits and self-care practices, it is important to lead by example. As educators, mentors, and role models, it is important to practice what we preach and demonstrate healthy habits and self-care practices in our own lives. By modeling healthy behaviors and self-care practices, we can inspire and motivate others to prioritize their own well-being. Leading by example can help create a culture of health and wellness within our communities and empower others to make positive changes in their own lives. By promoting a balanced lifestyle, prioritizing mental and emotional well-being, cultivating positive relationships, and leading by example, we can help individuals develop the skills and strategies needed to navigate life's challenges with resilience and grace. By instilling healthy habits and self-care practices early on, we can empower individuals to take control of their health and well-being and create a life that is vibrant, joyful, and fulfilling.

- Building resilience through physical health

Building resilience through physical health is a crucial aspect of overall well-being and is essential for maintaining a strong and robust mindset in the face of adversity. Resilience refers to the ability to bounce back from difficult situations and challenges, and physical health plays a vital role in supporting this resilience. When our bodies are in good physical condition, we are better equipped to handle stress, overcome obstacles, and maintain a positive outlook on life.

One of the key ways in which physical health contributes to resilience is through the release of endorphins during exercise. Endorphins are neurotransmitters that act as natural painkillers and mood elevators, helping to reduce feelings of stress and anxiety. Regular physical activity has been shown to increase the production of endorphins, leading to improved mood and a greater sense of well-being. This can be especially beneficial during times of stress or hardship, as it can help to boost our mood and energy levels, making it easier to cope with challenging situations.

Furthermore, physical health is closely linked to mental health, and the two have a reciprocal relationship. When we take care of our physical health through regular exercise, healthy eating, and adequate sleep, we are better able to manage our mental health and emotional well-being. Research has shown that exercise can help to reduce symptoms of anxiety and depression, improve cognitive function, and enhance overall mental health. By prioritizing our physical health, we are setting a strong foundation for resilience in the face of adversity.

In addition to the benefits of exercise, maintaining good physical health also involves paying attention to other aspects of our well-being, such as nutrition and sleep. A balanced diet rich in fruits, vegetables, whole grains, and lean proteins provides us with the essential nutrients our bodies need to function optimally. Eating a healthy diet can help to regulate our mood, energy levels, and cognitive function, all of which are important factors in building resilience. Furthermore, getting an adequate amount of sleep is crucial for physical health and overall well-being. Sleep plays a vital role in the body's ability to repair and regenerate, as well as in the regulation of hormones that impact mood and stress levels. By prioritizing nutrition and sleep, we can support our physical health and enhance our resilience in the face of challenges.

Another important aspect of building resilience through physical health is developing healthy coping strategies for stress and adversity. When we encounter difficult situations or setbacks, it is natural to experience stress and negative emotions. However, how we respond to these challenges can greatly impact our ability to bounce back and persevere. Engaging in regular physical activity can be a powerful coping mechanism for managing stress and building resilience. Exercise has been shown to reduce levels of the stress hormone cortisol, improve cognitive function, and enhance emotional well-being. By incorporating physical activity into our daily routine, we can better equip ourselves to handle stress and adversity in a healthy and constructive manner. By taking care of our bodies and prioritizing our physical well-being, we can support our mental health, emotional well-being, and overall resilience in the face of challenges. Physical health plays a crucial role in helping us to bounce back from adversity, overcome obstacles, and maintain a positive outlook on life. By incorporating regular physical activity, healthy eating habits, and stress management techniques into our daily lives, we can build a strong foundation for resilience and well-being. It is important to remember that resilience is a skill that can be cultivated and strengthened over time, and a focus on physical health is an essential component of this process.

Chapter 18: Navigating relationships and communication

- TEACHING BOYS EFFECTIVE communication skills

Teaching boys effective communication skills is a crucial aspect of their development and growth into well-rounded individuals. In today's fast-paced and interconnected world, the ability to communicate effectively is more important than ever. Boys, like all individuals, need to be equipped with the necessary tools and skills to express themselves clearly, engage in meaningful conversations, and build positive relationships with others. By teaching boys effective communication skills from a young age, we can help them navigate various social and professional situations with confidence and success.

One of the key components of teaching boys effective communication skills is helping them understand the importance of active listening. Active listening involves not just hearing words but also fully engaging with the speaker, understanding their perspective, and responding thoughtfully. Boys often struggle with active listening, as they may be more inclined to focus on their own thoughts and opinions rather than truly listening to others. By emphasizing the importance of listening in communication, we can help boys become more attentive and empathetic communicators.

Another important aspect of teaching boys effective communication skills is helping them develop their verbal and nonverbal communication abilities. Verbal communication involves the use of words to convey thoughts, feelings, and ideas, while nonverbal communication includes gestures, facial expressions, and body language. Boys may benefit from guidance on how to express themselves clearly and confidently through both verbal and nonverbal means. By encouraging boys to pay attention to their tone of voice, body posture, and facial expressions, we can help them convey their messages effectively and connect with others on a deeper level.

In addition to verbal and nonverbal communication, teaching boys effective communication skills should also focus on writing skills. Writing is a fundamental aspect of communication, and boys need to be able to express their thoughts and ideas clearly and cohesively in written form. By teaching boys how to organize their thoughts, structure their writing, and communicate their ideas effectively, we can help them succeed academically and professionally. Writing skills are essential in a wide range of contexts, from academic assignments to professional emails, and boys who are proficient writers will have a distinct advantage in many areas of their lives.

Furthermore, teaching boys effective communication skills should also involve helping them develop social communication abilities. Social communication involves interacting with others in a variety of social settings, from casual conversations to formal presentations. Boys may need guidance on how to navigate social interactions, build rapport with others, and communicate respectfully and effectively in different contexts. By providing boys with opportunities to practice their social communication skills, such as through group activities, role-playing scenarios, and public speaking exercises, we can help them become more confident and competent communicators.

Moreover, teaching boys effective communication skills should also incorporate digital communication skills. In today's digital age, boys are constantly communicating through various digital platforms, such as social media, email, and text messaging. It is important for boys to understand the nuances of digital communication, including how to convey tone and emotion effectively through written messages, how to maintain professionalism in online interactions, and how to navigate potential pitfalls such as cyberbullying and misinformation. By teaching boys how to communicate responsibly and respectfully in digital spaces, we can help them leverage the power of technology to connect with others and share their ideas. By focusing on active listening, verbal and nonverbal communication, writing skills, social communication, and digital communication, we can help boys develop the necessary tools and abilities to communicate confidently and effectively. By instilling in boys a strong foundation in communication skills, we can empower them to express themselves authentically, build positive relationships with others, and navigate various social and professional situations with confidence and success. Ultimately, teaching boys effective communication skills is an investment in their future growth and development as individuals who are able to communicate effectively, engage with others thoughtfully, and make a positive impact in the world.

- Building healthy relationships with family and friends

Building healthy relationships with family and friends is an essential aspect of a fulfilling and well-balanced life. Strong and positive relationships with those closest to us can provide emotional support, companionship, and a sense of belonging that can contribute to overall happiness and well-being. However, fostering and maintaining these relationships requires effort, communication, and mutual respect.

One key element to building healthy relationships with family and friends is effective communication. Open and honest communication is essential for resolving conflicts, addressing issues, and expressing thoughts and feelings. It's important to make an effort to listen actively, show empathy, and be willing to compromise or find solutions together. By communicating effectively, misunderstandings can be minimized, trust can be built, and relationships can flourish.

In addition to communication, mutual respect is a crucial component of healthy relationships. Respecting each other's boundaries, opinions, and feelings is essential for maintaining a positive and supportive connection. It's important to treat each other with kindness, understanding, and consideration, even in times of disagreement or conflict. By showing respect and consideration for one another, relationships can remain strong and resilient.

Another important aspect of building healthy relationships with family and friends is spending quality time together. Making an effort to connect and engage in meaningful activities can strengthen bonds and foster a deeper connection. Whether it's sharing meals, going for walks, or participating in shared interests, spending time together allows for shared experiences and memories that can create a sense of closeness and connection.

It's also important to show appreciation and gratitude for the people in our lives. Expressing thanks, acknowledging their efforts, and showing love and affection can help to nurture and deepen relationships. By showing appreciation and gratitude, we can create a positive and supportive environment that fosters strong and healthy relationships.

Furthermore, setting boundaries and boundaries is essential to maintaining healthy relationships with family and friends. It's important to communicate your needs, preferences, and limits clearly and assertively, while also respecting the boundaries of others. By establishing boundaries, we can create a sense of safety, respect, and trust within our relationships, which is essential for maintaining health and well-being.

Lastly, it's important to be willing to work through conflicts and challenges together in order to strengthen and maintain healthy relationships with family and friends. Conflict is a natural part of any relationship, and it's important to approach conflicts with compassion, empathy, and a willingness to find common ground. By addressing conflicts in a constructive and respectful manner, we can learn, grow, and develop a deeper understanding of each other, leading to stronger and healthier relationships. Effective communication, mutual respect, quality time together, appreciation, setting boundaries, and working through challenges are all key components to building and maintaining strong and healthy relationships. By prioritizing and nurturing these relationships, we can create a supportive and loving network of people who contribute to our well-being, happiness, and overall quality of life.

- **Empowering boys to navigate social situations**

Navigating social situations can be challenging for anyone, regardless of age or gender. However, for boys, in particular, there are unique challenges and pressures that they may face when it comes to social interactions. In today's society, there are certain expectations and stereotypes placed on boys, such as being strong, assertive, and independent. These stereotypes can sometimes make it difficult for boys to express their emotions, seek help, or show vulnerability in social situations. As a result, boys may struggle with developing healthy relationships, communicating effectively, and managing conflict in a constructive way. It is essential to empower boys to navigate social situations effectively, ensuring they have the skills and tools necessary to thrive in all aspects of their lives.

One important aspect of empowering boys to navigate social situations is teaching them emotional intelligence. Emotional intelligence refers to the ability to recognize, understand, and manage one's emotions, as well as to recognize and understand the emotions of others. By developing emotional intelligence, boys can better regulate their emotions, communicate effectively, and empathize with others. This can help them navigate social situations with confidence and ease, as they will be better equipped to handle conflicts, express their feelings, and build positive relationships. Teaching boys emotional intelligence can also help break down traditional gender stereotypes that suggest boys should be stoic and unemotional, encouraging them to embrace their emotions and express them in a healthy way.

Another important aspect of empowering boys to navigate social situations is teaching them effective communication skills. Communication is key in any social interaction, and boys need to learn how to express themselves clearly, listen actively, and negotiate conflicts peacefully. By teaching boys how to communicate assertively yet respectfully, they can build stronger relationships with their peers, parents, and teachers. Effective communication skills can also help boys navigate tricky social situations, such as peer pressure, bullying, or disagreements with friends. By empowering boys with the tools to communicate effectively, they can navigate social situations with confidence and assertiveness, ensuring they can advocate for themselves and others in a positive and respectful manner.

In addition to emotional intelligence and communication skills, another crucial aspect of empowering boys to navigate social situations is teaching them conflict resolution skills. Conflict is inevitable in any social interaction, and boys need to learn how to navigate disagreements and disputes in a constructive and respectful way. By teaching boys conflict resolution skills, they can learn how to identify issues, listen to different perspectives, and collaborate to find a solution that works for everyone involved. Conflict resolution skills can also help boys manage their emotions during conflicts, avoid escalating situations, and build stronger and more resilient relationships. By empowering boys with the skills to resolve conflicts peacefully, they can navigate social situations with confidence and poise, ensuring they can handle any challenge that comes their way.

Furthermore, it is essential to empower boys to navigate social situations by teaching them about empathy and building healthy relationships. Empathy is the ability to understand and share the feelings of others, and it is a critical skill for navigating social situations. By teaching boys empathy, they can develop a deeper understanding of others, show compassion and kindness, and build stronger connections with their peers. Empathy can help boys navigate social situations by allowing them to see things from different perspectives, recognize the feelings and needs of others, and respond with care and understanding. By fostering empathy in boys, we can help them build healthy relationships based on trust, respect, and mutual support, ensuring they can navigate social situations with empathy and integrity. By teaching them emotional intelligence, communication skills, conflict resolution skills, and empathy, boys can develop the tools and confidence they need to thrive in all aspects of their lives. It is essential to break down gender stereotypes and encourage boys to embrace their emotions, express themselves assertively, and build healthy relationships. By empowering boys with the skills and mindset to navigate social situations effectively, we can help them become confident, compassionate, and resilient individuals who can navigate any social challenge with grace and dignity.

Chapter 19: Exploring opportunities for growth and development

- PROVIDING RESOURCES and support for boys with dyslexia

When it comes to providing resources and support for boys with dyslexia, it is essential to first understand what dyslexia is and how it impacts individuals. Dyslexia is a learning disorder that affects a person's ability to read, write, and spell. It is not a sign of low intelligence or laziness, but rather a specific learning difference that affects the way the brain processes information. Boys with dyslexia may struggle with decoding words, fluency, spelling, and reading comprehension, which can impact their academic performance and self-esteem.

One of the key resources that can support boys with dyslexia is early identification and intervention. Research has shown that early intervention can greatly improve outcomes for children with dyslexia by providing targeted support and strategies to help them overcome their challenges. Schools and parents play a crucial role in identifying dyslexia in boys and ensuring they receive the support they need. This can involve screening for dyslexia, conducting comprehensive assessments, and developing individualized education plans to address their specific needs.

Another important resource for boys with dyslexia is specialized instruction and support in the classroom. Teachers can implement evidence-based instructional methods and accommodations to help boys with dyslexia succeed academically. This may include using multisensory techniques, providing extra time for reading and written assignments, and using assistive technology to support their learning. In addition, boys with dyslexia can benefit from small group instruction and personalized learning plans to meet their unique needs and learning styles.

In addition to academic support, boys with dyslexia may also benefit from social and emotional support to help them navigate the challenges of living with a learning disorder. Dyslexia can impact a child's self-esteem, confidence, and social relationships, so it is important to provide them with resources and strategies to cope with these challenges. This may involve counseling, peer support groups, and social skills training to help boys with dyslexia build resilience and develop positive coping mechanisms.

Parental involvement and support are also crucial resources for boys with dyslexia. Parents play a key role in advocating for their child's needs, collaborating with teachers and school staff, and providing emotional support at home. By educating themselves about dyslexia, connecting with other parents of children with dyslexia, and seeking out resources and support services, parents can help their son succeed in school and in life. This may involve attending parent workshops, joining support groups, and staying informed about best practices for supporting children with dyslexia. By identifying dyslexia early, implementing evidence-based instructional methods, providing social and emotional support, and involving parents in the process, we can create a supportive and inclusive environment for boys with dyslexia to thrive. Together, we can empower boys with dyslexia to succeed academically, build confidence, and achieve their goals.

- Encouraging boys to pursue their interests and passions

It is important to encourage boys to pursue their interests and passions in order to help them develop into well-rounded individuals with a strong sense of self-confidence and purpose. Boys often face societal pressures to conform to traditional gender norms and expectations, which can lead them to suppress their true interests and passions in favor of activities that are considered more "masculine." However, it is crucial to remember that every individual is unique and has their own unique talents and passions that should be nurtured and supported.

One way to encourage boys to pursue their interests and passions is to create a supportive environment where they feel free to express themselves without fear of judgment or ridicule. This can be achieved by encouraging open communication and creating a safe space for boys to explore their interests and try new things. By listening attentively to their thoughts and feelings, parents and educators can help boys identify their passions and provide the necessary support and guidance to help them pursue their dreams.

Furthermore, it is important to expose boys to a variety of activities and experiences that can help them discover their interests and passions. This can involve enrolling them in extracurricular activities such as sports, music, art, or theater, or encouraging them to explore different hobbies and interests on their own. By exposing boys to a diverse range of experiences, they can discover what truly excites and motivates them and begin to pursue those interests with passion and dedication.

In addition, it is essential to provide boys with positive role models who can inspire and encourage them to pursue their interests and passions. This can involve introducing them to successful individuals in their chosen field of interest, as well as supporting their efforts to connect with mentors and peers who share their passions. By surrounding boys with positive influences who believe in their potential and encourage them to follow their dreams, we can help them build the confidence and resilience they need to overcome obstacles and achieve their goals.

It is also important to teach boys the value of hard work, perseverance, and dedication in pursuing their interests and passions. Developing a strong work ethic and a willingness to put in the time and effort required to excel in their chosen field can help boys overcome challenges and obstacles and stay motivated in the face of setbacks. By instilling a sense of discipline and determination in boys from an early age, we can help them develop the necessary skills and mindset to pursue their passions with confidence and resilience.

Furthermore, it is important to support boys in setting achievable goals and milestones that can help them track their progress and stay motivated in pursuing their interests and passions. By breaking down their larger goals into smaller, manageable tasks, boys can stay focused and on track as they work towards achieving their dreams. Celebrating their successes and acknowledging their efforts along the way can also help boys build a sense of accomplishment and confidence in pursuing their interests and passions. By creating a supportive environment, exposing them to diverse experiences, providing positive role models, teaching them the value of hard work and dedication, and supporting them in setting achievable goals, we can empower boys to follow their dreams and pursue their passions with passion and determination. By nurturing their unique talents and interests, we can help boys build the skills and mindset they need to thrive in their chosen field and lead fulfilling and meaningful lives.

- Building a roadmap for lifelong success

Building a roadmap for lifelong success is a crucial endeavor that requires careful planning, dedication, and resilience. It involves setting long-term goals, identifying key milestones, and staying committed to personal growth and development over the course of one's life. Success is often viewed as a journey rather than a destination, and having a roadmap can help individuals navigate the ups and downs of life with greater clarity and purpose.

One of the first steps in building a roadmap for lifelong success is to define what success means to you personally. This may involve reflecting on your values, passions, and aspirations, and formulating a vision for your future self. Success is a subjective concept that can vary greatly from person to person, so it's important to take the time to consider what success looks like for you and what you hope to achieve in your lifetime.

Once you have a clear idea of what success means to you, the next step is to set specific, measurable, achievable, relevant, and time-bound goals, also known as SMART goals. These goals should be aligned with your vision of success and serve as a roadmap for the steps you need to take to achieve it. By breaking down your long-term goals into smaller, manageable milestones, you can create a roadmap that outlines the path to success and helps you stay focused and motivated along the way.

In addition to setting goals, it's important to cultivate a growth mindset and embrace lifelong learning and development. Success is not a static state but a dynamic process that requires continuous adaptation and growth. By staying curious, open-minded, and willing to learn from both successes and failures, you can build the resilience and agility needed to overcome challenges and seize opportunities for growth and development.

Another key component of building a roadmap for lifelong success is to cultivate a strong support network of mentors, peers, and advisors who can provide guidance, feedback, and encouragement along the way. Success is rarely achieved in isolation, and having a supportive community of like-minded individuals can help you stay accountable, motivated, and connected to your goals and aspirations.

It's also important to prioritize self-care and well-being as you pursue lifelong success. Maintaining a healthy work-life balance, practicing self-care activities, and nurturing your physical, emotional, and mental health are essential for long-term success and fulfillment. By prioritizing self-care and well-being, you can ensure that you have the energy, resilience, and clarity of mind needed to stay focused and productive on your journey to success. By defining what success means to you, setting SMART goals, cultivating a growth mindset, building a strong support network, and prioritizing self-care and well-being, you can create a roadmap that guides you towards a fulfilling and successful life. Success is a journey, not a destination, and by embracing the challenges and opportunities that come your way, you can continue to grow and evolve throughout your lifetime.

Chapter 20: Conclusion

- **REFLECTING ON THE** journey of raising resilient sons with dyslexia

Raising a child with dyslexia can present unique challenges and opportunities for growth. As a parent of a son with dyslexia, it is important to reflect on the journey of raising a resilient child who can thrive despite their learning differences. The term "resilient" refers to the ability to recover or adjust to adversity and challenges, and it is a critical trait for children with dyslexia to develop in order to navigate a world that may not always be understanding or supportive of their needs.

One key aspect of raising resilient sons with dyslexia is to provide them with the tools and resources they need to succeed. This can include access to specialized education and interventions, such as Orton-Gillingham tutoring or assistive technology, as well as emotional support and encouragement from their parents and teachers. By giving your son the tools he needs to overcome his challenges, you are helping him build a strong foundation for resilience.

Additionally, it is important to foster a growth mindset in your son, encouraging him to view his dyslexia as a challenge to be overcome rather than a barrier to success. By emphasizing the importance of hard work, perseverance, and self-advocacy, you can help your son develop the skills and mindset needed to take on challenges and setbacks with a positive attitude and a determination to succeed.

Another key aspect of raising resilient sons with dyslexia is to cultivate a supportive and understanding environment at home and at school. This can include advocating for your son's needs with teachers and school administrators, as well as creating a safe and nurturing space where he feels comfortable expressing his feelings and asking for help when needed. By creating a supportive environment, you are helping your son build a strong sense of self-esteem and self-efficacy, which are essential components of resilience.

It is also important to model resilience for your son, showing him that setbacks and challenges are a natural part of life and that it is possible to overcome them with hard work and determination. By demonstrating resilience in your own life, you are teaching your son valuable lessons about perseverance, resilience, and the importance of never giving up on your dreams. By providing your son with the tools, resources, and support he needs to succeed, cultivating a growth mindset, creating a supportive environment, and modeling resilience in your own life, you can help your son develop the skills and mindset needed to thrive despite his learning differences. Remember, every child is unique, and what works for one child may not work for another. It is important to tailor your approach to suit your son's individual needs and abilities, and to never lose sight of the incredible potential and strengths that lie within him. By nurturing your son's resilience and helping him develop a positive self-image, you are setting him on a path to success and fulfillment in all aspects of his life.

- Celebrating the progress and growth of boys

Throughout history, boys have often been expected to embody certain traits and behaviors that align with traditional notions of masculinity. From a young age, they are taught to be strong, assertive, and independent. However, it is important to recognize that each boy is unique and may not fit into these narrow stereotypes. As society becomes more inclusive and understanding of diverse identities, it is crucial to celebrate the progress and growth of boys in a way that reflects their individuality and encourages them to embrace their true selves.

One key aspect of celebrating the progress and growth of boys is acknowledging the importance of emotional intelligence. Boys are often socialized to suppress their emotions and prioritize stoicism over vulnerability. This can have negative consequences on their mental health and overall well-being. By encouraging boys to explore and express their emotions in healthy ways, we can help them develop a deeper understanding of themselves and others. This in turn can lead to stronger relationships, better communication skills, and enhanced problem-solving abilities.

Another important way to celebrate the progress and growth of boys is by recognizing and valuing their unique interests and talents. Boys should not be confined to rigid gender roles that limit their potential. Instead, they should be encouraged to pursue their passions and explore a wide range of activities, regardless of whether they are traditionally considered "masculine" or "feminine. " This can help boys develop a strong sense of self-confidence and self-worth, as well as cultivate a sense of curiosity and open-mindedness.

In addition to emotional intelligence and individual interests, it is essential to celebrate the progress and growth of boys by supporting their academic and personal development. Boys may face specific challenges in school, such as a higher likelihood of being diagnosed with learning disabilities or behavioral issues. It is important to provide boys with the resources and support they need to succeed academically, whether that involves additional tutoring, counseling, or accommodations in the classroom. By recognizing and addressing these challenges, we can help boys reach their full potential and excel in all areas of their lives.

Furthermore, celebrating the progress and growth of boys also means promoting positive masculinity and healthy relationships. Boys should be taught to respect themselves and others, to communicate effectively, and to resolve conflicts peacefully. By fostering a culture of mutual respect and understanding, we can help boys develop strong interpersonal skills and build meaningful connections with their peers and mentors. This can also contribute to creating safer and more inclusive communities where all individuals can thrive. By encouraging boys to explore their emotions, pursue their interests, excel academically, and cultivate positive relationships, we can help them become confident, compassionate, and resilient individuals. It is crucial to recognize the unique strengths and abilities of boys and empower them to embrace their true selves. Through this approach, we can create a more inclusive and supportive environment where boys can thrive and contribute positively to society.

- Looking ahead to a bright and successful future

When looking ahead to a bright and successful future, it is important to have a clear vision of your goals and aspirations. Setting specific and achievable objectives can help guide your actions and keep you focused on the path to success. Whether you are starting a new business, pursuing a higher education degree, or seeking personal growth and development, having a roadmap for the future can greatly increase your chances of achieving your dreams.

One key aspect of planning for a successful future is identifying and leveraging your strengths. By understanding your unique abilities and talents, you can make informed decisions about the direction you want to take and the steps you need to take to get there. Additionally, recognizing areas where you may need to improve or seek additional support can help you develop a plan for growth and development.

Another important factor in looking ahead to a bright and successful future is maintaining a positive mindset. It is easy to become discouraged when faced with challenges or setbacks, but by focusing on the potential for growth and learning in every situation, you can maintain a sense of optimism and resilience. Surrounding yourself with supportive and positive influences can also help you stay motivated and inspired on your journey towards success.

In addition to personal growth and development, it is also important to consider the external factors that may impact your future success. This could include changes in the economy, advancements in technology, or shifts in the job market. By staying informed about trends and developments in your field, you can better prepare for potential opportunities or challenges that may arise. Additionally, building a strong network of contacts and mentors can provide valuable support and guidance as you navigate the ever-changing landscape of the professional world.

Ultimately, looking ahead to a bright and successful future requires a combination of self-awareness, goal setting, positive mindset, and strategic planning. By taking the time to assess your strengths and weaknesses, set clear objectives, and remain adaptable to change, you can position yourself for growth and success in the years to come. Remember that success is not defined by a single achievement, but rather by the journey of growth and learning that leads you towards your ultimate goals. With dedication, perseverance, and a willingness to take risks, you can create a future that is both fulfilling and successful.